"Not often do I come across a b[ook that] me with conviction in painful [...] on pastoring, in light of Jesus' words for the seven churches in Revelation, are wise, measured, and profound, applying the heart of the gospel to the heart of the pastor."

—TREVIN WAX,
vice president for research and resource development at the
North American Mission Board; visiting professor at
Cedarville University; author of *The Thrill of Orthodoxy*,
The Multi-Directional Leader, and *This Is Our Time*

"For a host of reasons, the feeling of weariness has reached a fever pitch in recent days. What better time than now for a meaningful, life-giving, hope-filled reflection on Jesus' answer to weariness to be shared with the world. In *Jesus Is Enough*, Jeremy has provided such a reflection. For all who are eager to see and savor the rest-giving attributes of Jesus afresh, I highly recommend this book."

—SCOTT SAULS,
senior pastor, Christ Presbyterian Church;
author of *Jesus Outside the Lines* and *Beautiful People Don't Just Happen*

"Pastoring is a hard job. There are so many aspects of this calling that go virtually unseen by the watching world, and yet carry great emotional and spiritual weight. It seems there's an increasing number of us keeping one eye on the door in case it gets to be too much. Nothing will make this calling easy, but this book offers great hope and help for navigating the path and walking in truth. If you're a pastor, whether you're feeling burnt out or not, you should read this book. It will help you if you're struggling, and it will prepare you for when later struggles come."

—RUSS RAMSEY,
pastor and author of *Rembrandt Is In the Wind:
Learning to Love Art Through the Eyes of Faith*

"In *Jesus Is Enough*, Jeremy addresses pastoral idolatries head-on: personal reputation, ministry metrics, doctrinal correctness, church influence, and more. He helps leaders take humbling inventory of our own temptations, while also inspiring us to build our worth and ministry on the incomparable sufficiency of Jesus. Like a best man in a wedding, this book urges us to not steal the bride's attention, but to rejoice in her attentiveness to the great Groom. I believe God will use this book to diminish petty pastoral idolatries and increase our estimation and enjoyment of Jesus Christ."

—JONATHAN DODSON,
author, *The Unwavering Pastor*

"Jeremy is writer for our times, with a work that speaks deeply to the hearts of pastors who are trying to faithfully shepherd in a pandemic shaped world. Using the seven churches of Revelation as a unique backdrop, *Pastor, Jesus Is Enough* grounds the difficult vocation of all pastors in the sufficiency of Christ and the hope of the gospel. A timely read for our challenging times."

—RONNIE MARTIN,
lead pastor of Substance Church in Ashland, Ohio, cohost of *The Happy Rant Podcast*, and coauthor of *Pastoring Small Towns*

"Rich with insight, *Pastor, Jesus Is Enough*, is a beautiful reminder that the self-worth of the pastor lies not in their occupation but in the person of Jesus. Writebol provides the reader with the helpful perspective of seeing Jesus as the hero of the pastor's life and church. Jesus is not impressed with our resume or our efforts to promote ourselves about the name of Jesus. This book will be helpful to any pastor seeking a renewed perspective of the love of Jesus."

—JIMMY DODD,
founder and president, PastorServe; author of *Survive or Thrive,
Six Relationships Every Pastor Needs*; *Pastors Are People Too*;
What Great Ministry Leaders Get Right;
and *The Magnificent Names of Jesus*

"The pressure of pastoring has rarely been greater than it is today. Jeremy reminds us that there is hope and comfort for the weary soul. This is a must read for every pastor who is being crushed under the weight of unrealistic expectations. The Good News is and has always been that Jesus is enough for his church, both shepherds and sheep."

—CHRIS BROOKS,
senior pastor, Woodside Bible Church

"Pastoral work has always had its challenges, those challenges have only increased in a post-Covid world. In this timely book, Jeremy Writebol, tenderly reminds those in ministry of the one thing we can never forget: Jesus is enough."

—BRIAN BRODERSEN,
pastor, Calvary Chapel Costa Mesa, CA

"Pastors matter to God. One clear evidence is when he raises up compassionate and compelling messages that speak with enduring relevance to the possibilities and perils of our call. *Jesus Is Enough* is one such message! Jeremy Writebol has done a great service to church leaders by offering this fascinating and timely study of Christ's words in Revelation to pastors. May we all experience the resilience and renewal for which this book was written!"

—DAVE HARVEY,
president of Great Commission Collective; author of
When Sinners Say I Do, The Plurality Principle, and *Stronger Together!*

"Building on the ancient words of Jesus to seven pastors, Jeremy Writebol brings necessary biblical clarity to the job description of today's pastors and challenges them to fulfill it through the sufficiency of Christ. Fresh, insightful, honest, and necessary—a must read!"

—DOUG SCHMIDT,
former senior pastor of Woodside Bible Church;
executive director of Barnabas Ministries of Michigan

"Ministry in Jesus' name has never been easy, and it seems to be growing harder. The ancient trifecta of devil, world, and flesh against us continues. But today's cultural decay, social turmoil, and political vitriol have ramped things up a notch—pastors are clearly an endangered species. Jeremy Writebol knows that firsthand. But he's learned that though he doesn't have what it takes to lead a church through times of tumult, Jesus does. Jesus is enough, Writebol reminds us, so quit trying to make ministry all about you. This book is chock full of biblical, practical wisdom for faithful ministry in this increasingly faithless era. Take and read; the soul you save may be your own."

—HAROLD L. SENKBEIL,
author of *The Care of Souls*

PASTOR, JESUS IS ENOUGH

HOPE FOR THE WEARY, THE BURNED OUT, AND THE BROKEN

PASTOR,
JESUS IS
ENOUGH

HOPE FOR THE WEARY, THE BURNED OUT, AND THE BROKEN

JEREMY WRITEBOL

FOREWORD BY JARED C. WILSON

LEXHAM PRESS

Pastor, Jesus Is Enough: Hope for the Weary, the Burned Out, and the Broken

Copyright 2023 Jeremy Writebol

Lexham Press, 1313 Commercial St., Bellingham, WA 98225
LexhamPress.com

Print ISBN 9781683596738
Digital ISBN 9781683596745
Library of Congress Control Number 2022945984

Lexham Editorial: Todd Hains, Jeff Reimer, Allie Boman, Mandi Newell, Jessi Strong
Cover Design: Brittany Schrock
Typesetting: Justin Marr

To Josh Carrillo and Paul Ortlinghaus,
fellow pastors and those "brothers of my heart"

CONTENTS

FOREWORD

P astoring churches is a weighty thing. It can also be an anxious thing. It is telling that in 2 Corinthians 11, after the apostle Paul has torn through a litany of afflictions and hardships that amount to his suffering for Christ—things like beatings and whippings, shipwrecks and assassination attempts, robbers and wild animals, starvation and hypothermia—he adds at the end of that list: "And, apart from other things, there is the daily pressure on me of my anxiety for all the churches" (v. 28).

I would add, just as a bit of applicational commentary, that *on top of all that* there is the frequent reality that a pastor must experience the daily pressure of this anxiety for the church *alone*. Or, at least, it often feels that way.

In 2021, we saw the first significant spike in years in the number of pastors who reported they were thinking about quitting. Over the last few years, the rank politicization of evangelicalism, the justice debates, the increasing balkanization among evangelical subcultures, and of course the coronavirus pandemic have all seemed to make shepherding even more weighty than it already was. I fear that in into the future, we'll begin to see more and more of our precious pastors crack under the weight of their anxiety for the church. What can be done?

Well, in 2 Corinthians 11:30–33, Paul directs us to embrace our weakness and rely on the rescuing hand of God. And this is exactly where Jeremy Writebol takes you in this book. Jeremy is not going to help you pretend your problems aren't real. He's not going to show you how to fake it until you make it. He's not going to puff you up with superficial inspiration that won't address the real challenges you face, the real burdens you bear, or the real power you have available to you. No, in *Pastor, Jesus Is Enough*, he is bluntly honest about that pressure, about that anxiety, about the fact that pastoring often hurts. But he also relentlessly points you to your only hope—the affectionate grace of Jesus, more abundant than all our afflictions.

Let Jeremy pastor you through these pages. Because shepherds need shepherds who have already walked the dark and winding path before them and can show them the way, who can in effect be a light. Whether you feel the weight of the last few years on your shoulders and are on the verge of packing it in, or whether you are just plodding through the regular pressure of anxiety for your church and need the encouragement of the gospel, you have a trustworthy friend in your hand.

Jared C. Wilson,
Kansas City, Missouri

PRAYER FOR
REST IN JESUS

In the name of the Father and of the Son and of the Holy Spirit. Amen.

> The LORD is my chosen portion and my cup;
> > you hold my lot.
> The lines have fallen for me in pleasant places;
> > indeed, I have a beautiful inheritance.   *Psalm 16:5–6*

> For you will not abandon my soul to Sheol,
> > or let your holy one see corruption.

> You make known to me the path of life;
> > in your presence there is fullness of joy;
> > at your right hand are pleasures forevermore.   *Psalm 16:10–11*

Almighty God, you have revealed your Son to us and blessed us through him. Grant that we may rest settled in him, never turning here or there, but as we entrust ourselves to his care be so satisfied with his all-sufficiency as our king and priest and mediator. Grant this so that among the many changes of this world our hearts may be fixed where true joys are found. By your mercy grant that we may offer ourselves as a living sacrifice, holy and acceptable to you. Through Jesus Christ our Lord. Amen.[1]

"JOHN TO THE seven churches that are in Asia:

"Grace to you and peace from him who is and who was and who is to come, and from the seven spirits who are before his throne, and from Jesus Christ the faithful witness, the firstborn of the dead, and the ruler of kings on earth.

"To him who loves us and has freed us from our sins by his blood and made us a kingdom, priests to his God and Father, to him be glory and dominion forever and ever. Amen. Behold, he is coming with the clouds, and every eye will see him, even those who pierced him, and all tribes of the earth will wail on account of him. Even so. Amen.

"'I am the Alpha and the Omega,' says the Lord God, 'who is and who was and who is to come, the Almighty.'

"When I saw him, I fell at his feet as though dead. But he laid his right hand on me, saying, 'Fear not, I am the first and the last, and the living one. I died, and behold I am alive forevermore, and I have the keys of Death and Hades.'"

REVELATION 1:4-8, 17-18

CHAPTER ONE

PASTOR, YOU BELONG TO JESUS

I t's exhausting, trying to be enough.

As our worship team opened our gathering with a welcome, my heart sank. The room was unusually quiet. Normally at least half the seats would be filled at the beginning of the service, with stragglers and those persistently behind showing up to fill the room by the time we had begun to sing the second or third song. But that dynamic had changed. On this particular Sunday there were maybe ten people in the room. The room that had been so full before was so, so silent.

I looked around wondering whether anyone else would show up. My heart hoped. A sea of troubles had crashed down on our congregation and on me as the pastor. I was defeated. Certainly, I had done my best to uphold the church. I wanted to see it be vibrant in its witness and work. I was concerned that the church be faithful in obedience to the Word of God, vital in our love for each other and our neighbors, and—more than anything—be the Christ-centered body of grace that our world desperately needed. Following the lead of my pastoral mentors, I wanted to be patient where there was disagreement, careful and wise in decision-making that would serve the weak and weary. Where there was a need for correction and discipline in the church, I tried to wield the sword of the Spirit as a physician's scalpel, not a butcher's cleaver. And yet, I couldn't be enough.

When a few in the church took issue with some statements of solidarity and compassion with hurting racial minorities in our community over police brutality, the charges for the explosion were set. As I navigated the complaints and criticism alongside fellow elders of my church, we sought to address the hearts of these individuals who had so vehemently objected. Instead of being open to correction they revolted and took a significant number of attenders in the church with them. The church was cut in half.

On that first Sunday after I looked around the room, I saw how may people were absent, and my heart broke. I tried so hard to hold it all together. I had lived my life trying to be a faithful, wise, and compassionate pastor. I gave every effort to lead well. And it was all gone. For five years I had seen the trajectory of the church move upward in all the "measurable categories." Attendance grew every year. We were on the brink of making plans for a building expansion or even relocation to a larger facility. Baptisms and conversions were frequent, membership was increasing, giving was abounding, leaders were multiplying, small groups growing, staff was being hired. All the best stuff of ministry was taking place. And within fewer than six months all the victories seemed to be wiped out. Some remained, but what had become of my beautiful church?

The psalmist's words, "Unless the LORD builds the house, those who build it labor in vain," echoed in my mind (Ps 127:1). Had I built in vain? Had I preached, served, discipled, prayed with, blessed, encouraged all for nothing? I compared myself to the couple John Piper warned about who wasted their lives collecting seashells.[2] At least they had the seashells. I had the remnant of a relationally bombed-out church. Shame washed over me because I was the leader. This wasn't supposed to happen under my watch. I *wasn't* enough.

Pastor, you aren't enough either.

I don't say that to be demeaning or to discount your accomplishments or faithfulness in ministry. I'm not trying to compare us, as if to say, "I couldn't be enough, so why in the world would you think you could be?" I'm trying to express the truth the Bible often draws out about how sufficient we are for the calling and work of ministry. Even the apostle Paul asked, "Who is sufficient for these things?" (2 Cor 2:16). And he was the apostle Paul. So we shouldn't think we are the exception. We aren't enough. We were never meant to be.

Our frustrations with this reality boil over from our own ambitions and perceptions and even definitions of what success in ministry should be. We want to pastor and lead well, so that the church will grow, and the measurable stuff of ministry will bloom all around us. Any setback, deficiency, or call for assistance makes us vulnerable to the charge of failure. We're like a small child wanting to be independent, shouting at their parent, "I can do it!"

I am not enough. You are not enough. Gratefully, our Savior Jesus, whom we serve, knows this. Here's how I know.

In 2018 the multisite church that I pastor began going through a significant leadership transition. Our senior pastor of over twenty-five years had announced his intentions to transition out of leadership, and the church would begin looking for his successor. As part of the transition strategy, Pastor Doug wanted to ensure that our church would avoid organizational drift away from our foundations both in mission and in method. Resources on mission drift were secured and supplied to all the staff and elders. As part of the team that identifies and shapes what each of our congregations would be hearing on Sunday mornings in the pulpit, I suggested a study on Revelation 2–3 and Jesus' letters to the churches. In my mind each of these letters identified a specific caution that Jesus would give to the churches and a way forward for them. It was a perfect series to call us to greater fidelity as a church and faithfulness in avoiding moral, theological, and methodological drift. However, I failed to account for one thing in my recollection of the content of Revelation 2–3: the pastors.

Where I had thought of each of these letters as an indictment against the church (mostly) and a solution (repentance) to fix what ailed them, I failed to see that there was a person looming large over the churches speaking directly to the leaders. His words, in fact, were the content of the letters to each church, but he wasn't speaking as a detached or distant CEO giving pragmatic instruction on how to fix a branch or two of the spiritual franchises. And it wasn't Jesus just tossing out leadership memos to these congregations about how to do better and try harder. He was writing to pastors. Real leaders, real individuals who were given the charge to lead local congregations in actual local communities. These letters are not Jesus' take on *The 7 Habits of Highly Effective People*.

When I saw the seven letters (and the entire book of Revelation for that matter) in this light, I realized Jesus was drawing close to suffering, insufficient, floundering pastors and churches. In the magnificence of his all-surpassing power and authority, he stands near pastors and churches to remind them of his ultimate victory over the cosmic powers that would undo them. In the triumph of the resurrection, he draws near as the "faithful witness, the firstborn from the dead and the ruler of the kings of the earth" (Rev 1:5 CSB). When he draws near to the apostle John on Patmos in Revelation 1, he appears in radiant glory. There is no question the vision of the resurrected, vindicated, glorified Jesus was to demonstrate his supreme and matchless authority over all contenders. If you're on the opposing side of his glory, you should be terrified. But if you're a "brother and partner in the affliction, kingdom, and endurance that are in Jesus," then Jesus showing up in glory for you is a welcome sight (Rev 1:9 CSB). He's truly the older brother coming to the rescue of his younger siblings being abused by a cowardly bully. In a cosmic sense, thinking about the universal church, that's really comforting. But there's a locality to this vision as well; don't miss it.

Seven cities are mentioned. Seven communities are identified as the places where Jesus' letter will land. John is commanded to "write what you see in a book and send it to the seven churches" Rev 1:11). While the number seven symbolizes the universal scope of this letter for all the churches, we can't look past the specific referents in Jesus' command to John. He has seven specific—in space and time—communities and churches in view. He shows up to say something to Ephesus and Smyrna and Pergamum and

Thyatira and Sardis and Philadelphia and Laodicea. He shows up to be something for these churches. He wants them to see that he is enough.

One element of the glorious visage of Jesus is described as a "mystery" that needs further explanation. John sees seven stars and seven golden lampstands. Jesus holds the seven stars in his right hand. He stands amid the seven lampstands. And without a point of reference, we're left to guess at what the significance of this placement is. Thankfully we're not left to speculate.

Jesus explains the mystery in this way: "The seven stars are the angels of the seven churches, and the seven lampstands are the seven churches" (Rev 1:20). Jesus stands in the midst of the churches; he holds the pastors in his right hand. Now it might seem a stretch to some to interpret these "angels" as pastors, but each of the following seven letters to specific local churches is written to the "angel" of that local church. If the stars or angels are not human individuals, it reduces the particular impact of how Jesus' glory is good news for specific communities and specific pastors in the midst of a hostile cultural context. I'm of the opinion (thankfully with others, notably Peter Leithart[3]) that Jesus isn't just speaking to some guardian angel or that the stars and angels are a spiritualized reference to the church. Plainly, the angel is a messenger, a pastor.

Jesus makes it plain where his attention is focused. He cares for his church. He's standing in the center of his people. Jesus cares for his pastors. They are held in his right hand. The letters are personal addresses from Jesus to these pastors about who he is and who they are. Underpinning every letter is the fact that the pastors are held in the dominant hand of authority and care of Jesus Christ himself. He begins each address confronting the pastors with a specific facet of his identity, directly pointed to the need and lack of "enoughness" that each pastor has. These letters are about how Jesus is enough for each of them, in their particular needs.

Make no mistake: Jesus will say hard words. He will confront sin and apathy. Jesus will get in the face of one or two and tell them they make him sick. He applies a healing word to the wounds of two pastors who are down on the mat after taking a beating from the enemy. Their weakness doesn't repel Jesus. He doesn't give up on any one of them.

He won't give up on you either. In fact, like Jesus' victorious promise to them, Jesus' expectation is that you will be victorious too. Yes: you, pastor. He's enough to see us home to the end. Each letter concludes with a promise and motivation to endure and press on trusting him. "To the one who conquers" (Rev 2:7) is an invitation to remember that we belong to Jesus and, "as I also conquered," so he will see to our victory as well (Rev 3:21).

These seven letters are love letters from Jesus to pastors, and the more I think about it, the more that seems right. Certainly, they aren't syrupy and sappy romantic letters, but they are nonetheless evidences of Jesus' care and concern for the pastors who lead his church. The introduction to the book of Revelation reminds us that it is from "him who loves *us* and has freed *us* from our sins by his blood" (Rev 1:5). These letters are the very Word of God for pastors today, like me and you, striving to be enough and yet forgetting to remember that we have a Savior who is absolutely enough. And you, pastor, belong to him!

So, because Jesus is enough, and because pastors belong to him, "let anyone who has ears to hear listen to what the Spirit says" Rev 2:7, 11, 17, 29; 3:6, 13, 22 CSB).

To the angel of the church in Ephesus write: "The words of him who holds the seven stars in his right hand, who walks among the seven golden lampstands.

"I know your works, your toil and your patient endurance, and how you cannot bear with those who are evil, but have tested those who call themselves apostles and are not, and found them to be false. I know you are enduring patiently and bearing up for my name's sake, and you have not grown weary. But I have this against you, that you have abandoned the love you had at first. Remember therefore from where you have fallen; repent, and do the works you did at first. If not, I will come to you and remove your lampstand from its place, unless you repent. Yet this you have: you hate the works of the Nicolaitans, which I also hate.

"He who has an ear, let him hear what the Spirit says to the churches. To the one who conquers I will grant to eat of the tree of life, which is in the paradise of God."

REVELATION 2:1-7

CHAPTER TWO

PASTORS LOVE JESUS THE MOST

"**M**inistry is a mistress."

Those words aren't only said by women who experience the neglect of being a pastor's wife while her husband in ministry is never home, always giving preference, energy, and time to the church, the staff, and those who have an "immediate need." The statement doesn't come exclusively from children who fail to see their father: who lose birthdays, vacations, and sports games to a dad who only has time for counseling the masses of his congregation, comforting the grieving in his flock, and caring about an invisible kingdom he's trying to build more than a family he was entrusted to serve.

In the quiet places of our hearts, many pastors will also say, "Ministry is a mistress." She's intoxicating, demanding, driving, exhilarating, unbearable, and unignorable. Ministry demands our best; it requires our peak focus and attention. We're inclined to think ministry, if it is going to bear fruit, is not a half-hearted weekend hobby we can give occasional attention to. We labor to preach excellent sermons, make disciples, comfort the hurting, encourage the faithful, build up the weak. And we like it! There is an adrenaline rush that kicks in when we are needed. Ministry demands may inconvenience our family, but that's part of the call, right? We get a prize in heaven for our sacrifices. We are tempted to believe the more we give up the greater our reward. And if we're honest, on most days, we actually love the whistle call of the saints demanding our attention.

Ministry is a mistress.

Would Jesus think so too? Could it be the one who called us to shepherd his people and share his gospel might be a little jealous of our affections towards his bride?

There's a knot I have to untangle when I think about the pastor's wandering affections and the "ministry mistress." On one hand, there are (usually) obvious signs when a pastor is in a ministry affair with his church. He's frantic. His pace is overwhelming. There is more and more and more and more he is trying to do for the kingdom of God. Ministry is an unquenchable fire that requires nearly everything from him. Early mornings, late nights, meeting to meeting to meeting defines his work. There is no quiet, no peace, no rest in his life. Taking a day off each week or using all his vacation time is sacrificed on the altar of "too much to do."

But in my experience, the pastor who is treating his church as a mistress is usually doing good work. He's not necessarily frayed at the edges trying to hold it all together. The pastor has found a way to be effective and successful in ministry and this has produced, from the outside, a healthy, sound, growing ministry. If he has any charisma or personal attractiveness, then people are all the more drawn to his work, which amplifies the problem. The pastor loves the ministry, the church wants his ministry, and an affair of the heart occurs.

When it comes down to it, Jesus isn't jealous of "the other man" trying to seduce his bride away from him. He's jealous to have the affections of the pastor himself. The pastor has a problem of disordered love, directing his heart and affections to another lover and away from the first love. Ministry, especially in its successes and victories, can seduce a pastor away from a true love for Christ and replace that love with a lesser love for ministry, approval, being needed, or a hundred other substitutes, so that what he does is to "love what it is wrong to love, or fail to love what should be loved, or love too much what should be loved less (or love too little what should be loved more)."[4]

THE ONE WHO HOLDS AND STANDS

In each Revelation letter sent to his pastors, Jesus gives them a specific view of himself. Each situation (or context) yields a distinct and specific self-revelation of God, a God who is transcendent over all and yet intimately involved in each context. Jesus didn't just create the church and then step back and let her get on with her mission apart from his presence and sovereign leadership. Jesus wants his pastors and churches to know him and experience his brilliance for his church.

Because of the repetition that occurs in the text from the end of chapter 1 to the first verse of chapter 2 we might be quick to skim over Jesus' presentation of himself. We've heard the line before, and its explanation, and we want to get on with what Jesus is going to say about the church in Ephesus. But the words Jesus says to Ephesus about who he is are not to be quickly passed over just because we've already heard them. The pastor at Ephesus needs to see Jesus in this way. The things that Jesus will address in the body of the letter have at their head a solution in who Jesus is. To pass over this is to miss the very remedy Jesus is offering to the pastor whose loves have become disordered.

The word to the pastor of the church in Ephesus comes from "him who holds the seven stars in his right hand, who walks among the seven golden lampstands" (Rev 2:1). Jesus is present in Ephesus. He's "intimately concerned with them," and his concern stems from the issues he is seeing in the church and more directly, in the very heart of the pastor.[5]

This pastor needs to see clearly that Jesus *walks among* the seven golden lampstands. He's not passively hovering on the fringes. He's active and busy in the churches. Not only is Jesus active in his church, but he also *holds* the stars in his right hand. More than just having them, the verb here reflects that Jesus is *grasping* his pastors in his hand. They aren't just there, they are held there. Again, it's an active sense of Jesus for his church, with his church, protecting his pastors and people. This pastor is being held securely in the hands of Jesus, as Jesus acts and works in his church.

Why is this vision of Jesus so important to start with? Because we often forget where he is and where we are. We go searching for approval and success in ministry, and our hearts are so disordered with love for the ministry that we forget the very one our ministry is to be all about. We're ignorant of the fact that Jesus is here in our church, and we're right there in his hand, and he is enough. But is that enough?

Jesus is this way for each of his pastors. He walks in your church, which is to say he is present in and among his people in active ways. We don't have to conjure up his presence to get something to happen. Jesus strides among his people. Jesus grasps you in his hand. Pastor, in Christ you are secure, protected, loved. Nothing is going to release you from his hand. You belong to Jesus and are held by Jesus. The best days may be ahead, the worst days may come, but Jesus has you right there in his hand.

ROTTEN RÉSUMÉS

If we're honest, we want our churches to be successful. Actually, if we are *human* we want our churches to be successful. We want our churches to grow both numerically and spiritually. We want to see a trajectory of life transformation and cultural impact from the result of the hours and hours of our labors. The successful pastor has to be a leader who actually has someone to pastor. And usually the more people to pastor, the more secure the ministry, the more established the reputation, the more successful the pastor.

The problem of the successful pastor or the successful church is the problem of underlined loves. In doing well as a pastor, or leading a flourishing church, we can find ourselves in the grip of loving the wrong things. Over the years of faithful, constant ministry, the affections of our hearts can shift from loving Jesus to loving the work. We can move from being passionately devoted to and in love with Jesus to being passionately devoted to and in love with our own ministries. The subtle shift that takes place is a shift, not of our affections, but in the object of our affections.

I imagine this is what happened with the church in Ephesus that we read about in Revelation 2:1–7. They were so focused on being a good church that their affections shifted from the Lord of the church to the work of the church itself.

There's no need to spend a lot of time telling you about Ephesus as a city or a church. When you look at the list of names of the leaders that pastored in Ephesus you don't have to guess whether they were a well-led, well-trained church. Leaders like Apollos,

Paul, Timothy, Titus, and even the beloved apostle John have been attributed with pastoring in Ephesus. Paul's farewell exhortation to the elders there to "pay careful attention to yourselves and to all the flock, in which the Holy Spirit has made you overseers" set the bar high for the culture of leadership in that church (Acts 20:28). Both the city and the church stood head and shoulders above every other community in Asia Minor.

From an external perspective, the work of the ministry in Ephesus was going very well. Even Jesus' letter commends them for their stalwart ministry. Jesus tells the pastor of the church that he knows "your works, your toil and your patient endurance" (Rev 2:2). Every pastor I know would like to have the résumé of Ephesus. Their character was high: "You cannot bear with those who are evil" (Rev 2:2). Their doctrine was sound, even discerning, rooting out false teachers. The church was especially faithful to Jesus in the midst of suffering and opposition. As a community they were poised for more success and stability. The church in Ephesus was the model kind of ministry that most of us would want today.

I want to be clear here; these attributes that Jesus affirms *are* worthy of affirmation. There is both much to commend and much we should avoid emulating in our ministries. At this point, Ephesus could be a paradigm or model for faithful success in ministry. The result of their ministry is aligned in many ways with what we would consider success. We will see in subsequent letters that holiness, sound doctrine, and perseverance in suffering are real outworkings of our belonging to Christ. When we see that Jesus is ours, that he is enough, and we are secure in him, then the vital shape of ministry is evident. As Harold Senkbeil puts it, a pastoral habitus is acquired that gives shape and form to our ministry.[6] If we are defining success in the ministry as faithfulness to Jesus, his Word, and his ways, then we will be successful when there is growing holiness, evident truthfulness, and humble suffering.

The danger comes when we make *our* definitions of success the ultimate goal.

If there is a problem in the pastorate today it is this: we are chasing bad definitions of success while measuring ourselves by these bad definitions, and we don't even realize we are missing the point. The church planter who has defined success by how many new congregations or campuses he can spin off from his initial plant is missing the point. The established church pastor who has defined success by holding the line for decades in an unwavering commitment to truth has missed the point. The savvy leader who has defined success by gaining access into the people and places of influence in our times has missed the point. The attractive and popular speaker with the beautiful-people music scene who has defined success by having a platform to speak to millions has missed the point. Even the pastor who has made the ultimate goal small, ordinary, everyday faithfulness in ministry has missed the point.

Jesus calls it out for us. "I have this against you, that you have left your first love" (Rev 2:4 NASB).

Jesus commends a church for their faithfulness to the ministry he has given them. But the pastor of Ephesus, in all his success, still has a big problem. Jesus still says, "I have this against you."

Pastor, here's a warning for us: Jesus won't be impressed at your résumé when you meet him. No matter how you've defined success, no matter what goal in ministry you've laid out for yourself, and whether you attain that goal or not, Jesus won't be impressed with your work. Our pursuits of holiness, truth, and perseverance are what faithful ministry looks like. But we can do all the faithful ministry in the world and still miss the ultimate goal of ministry. We could be the best preachers, counselors, leaders, multipliers, and ministry practitioners in the universe. Books could be written about our models of ministry, our biblical insight, our leadership savvy, and all the rest, and yet we can still miss the mark.

Jesus identifies the issue in Ephesus as lack of rightly ordered love, which affects the "good ministry" they were doing. Love for ministry has replaced love for Jesus who calls us to ministry. Love for the truth overshadows a love for Jesus, the Truth. Love for holiness is more evident than a love for Jesus, the Holy One. It's more desirable to be the one opposed and rejected one than to love the rejected Cornerstone. I shudder to think that many pastors would be perfectly happy if they were told they could have a successful ministry career without Jesus.

LOSING OUR FIRST LOVE

On a few occasions I've heard pastors confess sin to their congregation using the excuse, "I've lost my first love." Their moral and spiritual failure is named in the light of a loss of love. When the church is going through hard times of division and infighting, a guest minister will diagnose the issue before the congregation as a loss of their first love. This critique is usually given by, or about, or to the struggling pastor and his church. "Losing the first love" is the hidden cancer that lies under the surface of the exposed trouble and sin.

Ephesus wasn't a failing church. The pastor wasn't a morally duplicitous, spiritually anemic leader. He hadn't committed adultery with another woman in the church or embezzled funds from the weekly offering. He hadn't abandoned Christian orthodoxy and begun to teach heresy or water down the gospel with cultural syncretism. Holiness, discernment, and perseverance were the external characteristics of his ministry. What had happened was less morally wrong and more of a subtle exchange. He had traded the one thing necessary for a different, even good, thing (see Luke 10:38–42).

The danger is subtle. We don't abandon our first love overnight or in the spur of the moment. The loss of our first love is a gradual and sometimes imperceptible decline of our affections away from one thing and an increase of our affections for another. It's putting the spotlight on something good, while taking it off of something better.

Because of the subtle way our affections can be attracted, we can be unaware when a shift is happening in our hearts. The shift isn't always immediately apparent, but there are signals that can warn us of a definite reordering of our affections. Three particular shifts reveal a heart that has lost its first love.

FOCUS SHIFT: FROM JESUS TO ME

A major sign of a shift occurring in the heart of a pastor is what I'll call the "focus shift." Instead of ministry being about glorifying God and exalting Jesus, ministry becomes a means of putting a spotlight on the leader. This shift is often the result of ministry success. As the church grows and more lives are touched, the pastor can hear people affirming him. This isn't to say the affirmation is unwarranted or misplaced. But it's usually when the pastor begins to hear this affirmation, take it to heart, and especially desire it that the shift in his heart occurs. Pastors have to be careful about believing their own press and attributing to themselves the glory that belongs to the Lord.

The internal dialogue of a pastor undergoing this kind of shift is a kind of self-talk. He begins to write a narrative of his accomplishments and what he has done to grow and build the church. The leader becomes obsessed with protecting an identity of himself and believing that he is "the brand" of the church. If other gifted leaders begin to arise in the church, this pastor shows a shift in affections by sidelining the up-and-coming leaders, so they don't detract from his persona. Ministry isn't given or multiplied; it's siloed under the leader's platform. The pastor is the star of his church, with or without Jesus.

Even while proclaiming Christ and him crucified, the pastor has begun to shift the emphasis from the crucified Lord to his own intellect, her persuasiveness, his charisma, and his ability to gather people and bring in offerings. Jesus may get a mention or two, but the pastor who has lost his first love gradually has less and less to say about Jesus, and more and more to say about himself. There is an escalating emphasis on the pastor's vision and strategy. People are more and more called to sacrifice to fulfill his agenda for the success and scope of the church. He forgets his calling to shepherd and serve the flock of God with the Word of God and is more interested in the flock serving his agenda.

ATTITUDE SHIFT: FROM SERVING TO BEING SERVED

Not only is a pastor's focus an indicator of his affections, but so is his attitude. There can come a turn in a successful ministry when the pastor stops thinking about how to serve and care for the congregation, and how his congregation should be caring for and serving him. People and their needs are an interruption. The turn of the affections takes place when the pastor feels that he has given enough, and now it's his time to receive. He begins to believe that the church exists to support, serve, and steward his gifting and ministry. It's a departure from Jesus as our first love because Jesus himself "came not to be served but to serve, and to give his life as a ransom for many" (Mark 10:45).

When I start obsessively thinking about what my congregation should do to help promote me, my ministry, and my work, I know I'm experiencing a disordering of my loves. If I become irritable and angry with people because of how they do or don't advance my agenda or vision (even if it's only in my head), I know the shift is on. If there are things I won't do in ministry, people I won't serve in my church, and sacrifices I won't make, it could be because my love has shifted from Jesus to my own satisfaction.

Any time a pastor becomes the hero of his church, or the hero character of the ministry story, then a shift has occurred. The increasing literature and resources pointing out pastoral narcissism and abuse of power reflect a deep shift in the posture of leaders in ministry.[7]

POWER SHIFT: FROM PRAYERFUL DEPENDENCE TO MANUFACTURED RESULTS

We can note when our affections have shifted by asking where the results of our ministry efforts have come from. Ministry that is done in our own power, by our own hand and determination, is not ministry that comes from loving Jesus first. It's ministry that comes from our own love for ourselves and our success. The key sign of this shift is the shift away from a habit and life of prayer to "just doing it" in ministry work. For example, pastors who neglect prayer neglect the rich supply of grace in sitting at Jesus' feet and learning from him. Instead, they busy themselves—all in the name of serving Jesus— with things done on their own power and accord. Their love is for their results and what they have manufactured. Little idols of their own ministries stand, but their love for Jesus is diminished and cold.

Jesus told us, "Apart from me you can do nothing" (John 15:5). Yet we are more inclined to make things happen and be busy about ministry. Martin Luther is credited with remarking about his day being so full that he had to spend the first three hours in prayer.[8] Whether the story is apocryphal or not, the point is real, and this is what our calling demands. Pastors are to devote themselves to prayer (Acts 6:4)! The power shift occurs as we decline to rest in the power of the Spirit through prayer and insist working in the power of our own flesh to bring about success. We fail to believe that even the church is "made holy by the word of God and prayer" (1 Tim 4:5). We may see growth and movement in the church, but we won't find our hearts in love with Jesus.

When these shifts happen, we stop believing Jesus is enough for us. We deny that he is supremely lovely, worthy, and good. Instead, we are attracted away from a pure and sincere love for him. We forget that we are his blood-bought bride and that we belong to him. When we lose sight of him, we go looking for enoughness and belonging in the success of ministry. We're flirting with a ministry mistress that will never be able to fulfill our needs, satisfy our hearts, and captivate our affections with love.

CULTIVATING LOVE FOR JESUS

Because pastors belong to Jesus, they love Jesus the most.

That looks obvious, at least on paper. But we have the problem of losing our first love. Our relationship and passion for Jesus can be diminished by our reaction to our relative success in ministry.

Let me clarify that ministry success and ministry faithfulness are two different things. The externals of our work for the Lord—church growth, baptisms, growing budgets, larger influence and fame from an ever-expanding online audience, and similar metrics—are perhaps indicators of the reach of our ministry (and for some that equals success). But attaining these things does not require ministry faithfulness. Ministry faithfulness requires doing the work of pastoring and shepherding by the means and in the manner we are called to biblically. First Timothy 4:5 gives us a cue for the shaping dynamic of ministry faithfulness. Like everything else "created good," the church also is "made holy by the word of God and prayer." Jesus presents "the church to himself in splendor, without spot or wrinkle or any such thing" by the washing of the Word (Eph 5:26–27). The relationship between apostles and the proto-deacons in Acts 6 is a template for the function of ministry pastors are to prioritize today: prayer and the ministry of the Word. Pastors of the church are to dedicate themselves to these two dynamics above all.

Yet the call of ministry success can take us away from these practices. We can have ministry success without ministry faithfulness. Furthermore, we may believe that because we are experiencing some evidence of ministry success we are doing it the right way, and therefore being successful. It is in this space that our loves can become disordered.

If we want to keep our hearts and loves well-ordered, we must cultivate a life and ministry method that tethers us to what is of highest importance and is in keeping with Jesus as our first love. In the seasons of work when people are coming to Christ, the church is growing, budgets are solid, and speaking and itinerate ministry opportunities beyond our congregation abound, we must keep our hearts so that we aren't lured away by lesser loves. We have to keep our affections properly ordered.

At the point in my dating relationship when I began to say to my wife Stephanie, "I love you," she would ask (usually with a flirtatious grin), "Why?" We'd start playing a game where I would tell her reasons why my fascination and affection for her were growing. A little list would start to form of qualities and actions that drew me to her. I'd rehearse the list from time to time and watch her beam with delight at my observations. This practice was a means for me to think about Stephanie's qualities and characteristics that were attractive to me. It was a way for me to verbalize my affection and heart for her. Playing "How do I love thee? Let me count the ways" built up a language of love between us. It's a practice to keep my loves rightly ordered with my wife.

So how do we as pastors keep up our affections for Jesus? How do we cultivate a love for Jesus that supersedes all other loves?

Thankfully, the church is not in need of radical innovation or new invention to supply pastors with the means to cultivate and rightly order our loves. If we could turn the tables for just a moment and put ourselves in the seat of a member within our congregations coming to us for spiritual direction about our disordered loves, what spiritual practices would we *most likely* point them to? Regardless of what church tradition you come from, most of us would point to the two dynamics of ministry faithfulness above: receiving the cleansing Word of God and responding in prayer. James K. A. Smith puts it like this: "If the heart is like a compass ... then we need to (regularly) calibrate our hearts, tuning them to be directed to the Creator, our magnetic north. It is crucial for us to recognize that our ultimate loves, longings, desires and cravings are learned. And because love is a habit, our hearts are calibrated through imitating exemplars and being immersed in practices that, over time, index our hearts to a certain end."[9]

Our churches and traditions are rich in the resources to help even us pastors cultivate deeper and fuller love for Jesus amid the abundance of competing loves. While it may sound boring or even cliché to suggest that daily reflection in the Word of God and prayer are the means of cultivating love, especially when those practices can become mechanical and feel like going through the motions, few married couples would say that the constant presence and pursuit of their spouse toward them would be unwelcome. If anything, the regular giving of words of affirmation and affection, as well as showing up with real presence, would be the very practices to keep love aflame in a marriage.

I've become increasingly helped by higher liturgical traditions of keeping the Daily Office of Morning and Evening Prayer, specifically by the Anglican Book of Common Prayer. Not being an Anglican myself, I often looked with suspicion on the traditions that used (or even needed) prayer books to feed words into the soul for speaking to God. I had come to believe that re-praying the same things on a daily basis was the very kind of "empty phrases" Jesus warned against heaping up in Matthew 6:7. Yet year after year I would find myself desperately frustrated that I didn't possess the discipline to keep up with a read-the-Bible-in-one-year plan, find ways to impress the prayers of the Psalms into my heart, and give myself to praying for the right things at the right times every day. I had become good at ministry success externally, and even busy about doing the right work, but I was deficient in the interior resources of cultivating love for Jesus. I knew the accepted low-church formula of praying ACTS (Adoration, Confession, Thanksgiving, Supplication) was a helpful pattern, but I needed more than just a structure. I needed words to fit in that structure, and I was often frustrated and exhausted at trying to come up with my own.

When my brother-in-law shared with me a few years ago that his family had started attending an Anglican congregation in their area, it provoked a curiosity in me. At family holiday gatherings when we would stay over a few nights I noticed a copy of the Book of Common Prayer in the living room. I was intrigued but nothing more. Then the pandemic hit. I was out of sync, out of rhythm, out of words. Someone suggested I pick up the Daily Office of Morning and Evening Prayer.

The Book of Common Prayer became an invitation to ordering my affections through the Word and prayer every day. I found it didn't impose a new law of religious performance on me to tell me whether I was being successful; it invited me into the love of God through reciting and receiving the very Word of God and then responding back again with his Word in prayer. I was given daily language with which to confess my sins and disordered heart. I was reminded of the atoning work of Christ for my justification, sanctification, and ultimate glorification. The prayer book invited me into a rhythm of worship walking through sequences of remembering "sin, grace, and faith," which J. I. Packer calls "evangelical worship."[10]

My posture has changed from trying to succeed in checking off the boxes of reading the Bible daily to receiving the Word of Christ with faith each and every day. Instead of praying to pivot God into blessing my ambitions and plans, I now respond with love to him because he first loved me (1 John 4:19). The rhythm of cultivating love through receiving the Word and responding in prayer centers me on the gospel of God's love and allows me to live out of that love in my life.

I share this to invite you to the dynamics of spiritual renewal in being made holy by the Word and prayer. Whatever your tradition might be, the invitation the Lord makes to "stand by the roads, and look, and ask for the ancient paths, where the good way is; and walk in it, and find rest for your souls" is available (Jer 6:16). Whether through the practices of Morning and Evening Prayer, *lectio divina*, silence and solitude with the Word of God, or a daily "quiet time" of reading and praying through a read-the-Bible-in-one-year plan, we need the renewing and revitalizing washing of the Word to cultivate love for Christ within our hearts.

LEADING BY LOVING JESUS MOST

The seduction of ministry success doesn't just pull *us* away from Jesus. It can pull our churches away from Jesus.

John the Baptist gave me clarity on how to identify this role and what it looked like when his disciples approached him with the "problem" of his cousin's (Jesus') growing ministry and influence. Not too far from where John had been laboring in a successful ministry of his own, Jesus set up a baptismal ministry as well. It bothered John's disciples because it seemed they were losing influence and the crowds. They complained, "All are going to him" (John 3:26). But it didn't throw John the Baptist. We have no indication that he went off into the wilderness and stewed over the problem. He didn't come up with a new ministry strategy to recapture people who were on the fence and in-between. John had a rightly ordered love. He didn't see it as a loss on his part. They were all going to Jesus—as they should be!

John the Baptist was able to not lose a beat in pointing to Jesus because he understood who he was. His identity, spoken over him by the Word of God, was the one forerunner, going "before the Lord to prepare his ways, to give knowledge of salvation to his people in the forgiveness of their sins" (Luke 1:76–77). His illustration to the concerned disciples captures for me the identity we have in our relationship, as pastors, with Jesus. John put it like this: "The one who has the bride is the bridegroom. The friend of the bridegroom, who stands and hears him, rejoices greatly at the bridegroom's voice. Therefore this joy of mine is now complete. He must increase, but I must decrease" (John 3:29–30).

John's illustration is a wedding, a love story. On that commitment day, the groom and the bride make covenant vows of love to each other. In every wedding ceremony I've officiated, the couple can't take their eyes off each other. They are locked in gaze with one another. Yet, imagine the best man starts to attract the gaze of the bride. He flexes his muscles, winks at her, even blows kisses her way. He does all he can to flirt with her right there at the altar! Anyone with half a brain would conclude that this guy is a lousy friend, and woe to the marriage if the friend actually gets the attention of the bride and she sends back winks and kisses.

If the axiom "As the leaders go, so goes the church" is true, then if our loves are disordered between Jesus and the ministry, so can our church's loves be disordered. Even if the external metrics of attendance growth, ministry programs, spiritual transformation, volunteer serving, and financial soundness are there, Jesus could still say to us, "You've lost your first love." The reality is, we won't have true success if we love anyone or anything else more than

Jesus. As a pastor I have to think about my role in helping the church love Jesus most.

Pastors, when we try to take the church's eyes off the bridegroom Jesus and divert her attention our way, we are lousy friends of the groom. By the way we go about the work of ministry and the leading of our lives we can wrongly order the love of our church away from Jesus first and put her affections onto ourselves, our programs, our wisdom, our charisma, or anything else.

But the friend of the groom does something different. He rejoices greatly at the groom's voice. He makes sure the groom "increases" in the eyes of the bride. We have to remember we are the bride of Christ; our eyes should be fixed on him. We, as pastors, are the friends of the groom. He must increase, we must decrease. The way I like to say it with my staff, elders, deacons, deaconesses, and Sunday-morning worship team is this: "Let's put the spotlight on Jesus."

Leading by loving Jesus most is putting the spotlight on Jesus in all our ministry work. Leading by loving Jesus most is by putting the spotlight on him in all our affections and desires. Leading by loving Jesus most is by making sure that whoever we serve sees Jesus, not us.

LOVE ETERNAL, LOVE DIVINE

Jesus called the pastor of the church at Ephesus to repent. The loss of love for Jesus first and foremost, even while the success of the ministry abounded around him, was enough for Jesus to call out the spiritual adultery that was taking place right within their midst. As Jesus concludes his first letter to the church, he invites the universal church, you and me included, into this reflection: "Let anyone who has ears to hear listen to what the Spirit says" (Rev 2:7).

Pastor, are you listening? Having ears to hear, are you listening to the voice of Jesus who is calling for a reordering of your loves? As you consider your loves, are you more interested in loving the success you are attaining and the praise you are accumulating than you are in Jesus? Would Jesus affirm your faithfulness to the right things (doctrinal fidelity, ethical purity, endurance in suffering) and yet rebuke your displaced affections for the results of that work? Is he jealous that you love the ministry more than you love him?

"Let anyone who has ears to hear listen to what the Spirit says."

When we go looking for another lover or are attracted by the promises of other loves, we are buying into their promises. *Ministry* makes promises to us. It offers approval and applause. Ministry can be a place where power and prominence are found. It invites us to a world where we pastors are at the top. Climbing ecclesiastical leadership ladders and being affirmed for our great sermons, growing churches, and global notoriety is intoxicating. Ministry, in many ways, offers us love.

But so does Jesus. And his love is far greater and more solid and secure than the love this ministry life offers.

With every letter Jesus both gives a vision of who he is and a concluding promise "to the one who conquers." What Jesus offers to the pastor of Ephesus, and to us as pastors today, is nothing short of the eternal security, love, and affection of God himself. In symbolic language we are told the one who conquers will "eat of the tree of life, which is in the paradise of God" (Rev 2:7). This image reflects back to the very first pages of Scripture, envisioning the garden-paradise of Eden. There humanity enjoyed the security, provision, and presence of God in ineffable delight. Paradise with God was a place of full affirmation, devotion, and affection. The love we so deeply crave is found in the presence of God. The one who overcomes will partake of this eternal life in the presence of God, never to be broken again.

This may induce some anxiety about what it takes to overcome. Is Jesus affirming that only those who achieve ministry success will attain eternal approval? Are the only winners in the next life the ones who actually win in this life? Is it all contingent on my efforts to make it across the finish line? Reading the promise isolated from the context may yield that conclusion, but we're missing the bigger picture if that's what we determine.

As one pastor so beautifully stated it, "Because I am in Jesus, what is true of Jesus is true of me. What belongs to Jesus belongs to me."[11] We can believe this promise because Jesus has declared himself as the one who has overcome (John 16:33). Therefore, those who are in Christ have overcome and will overcome as well. John writes, "For everyone who has been born of God overcomes the world. And this is the victory that has overcome the world—our faith. Who is it that overcomes the world except the one who believes that Jesus is the Son of God?" (1 John 5:4–5). So, what is true of Jesus (he has overcome) is true of me (I have overcome).

In this we can consider the promise and what it means for pastors struggling with making ministry a mistress to whom we give our affection and devotion. All the affirmation and approval we seek, the love we so long to get back from the mistress of ministry, is ours and is coming for us. We have it now by virtue of the fact that we are gripped securely in the hand of Jesus. Pastor, nobody can rip you out of his loving embrace. And that same and fulfilled and eternal love we are eager to have is coming for us on the final day of consummation.

As a result, we have no business flirting with the mistress of ministry. The church may be where we work and labor for the sake of our greater love, Jesus. But the church is not the place where we should yield our highest love. The success of ministry may come. But that success cannot carry the ultimate fulfillment of what we already have in Christ. The joy of ministry may be great, but that joy cannot capture the ecstatic joy that Jesus offers us and the "pleasures forevermore" that are at *his* right hand (Ps 16:11).

Pastor, because we belong to Jesus, we can love Jesus most. We have no need to take ministry as a mistress. No need to leave our first love. Jesus is enough. We don't need the applause or approval of ministry success. Jesus is enough. We don't have to have disordered loves, abandoned families, or misplaced affections. Jesus is enough.

AND TO THE angel of the church in Smyrna write: "The words of the first and the last, who died and came to life.

"I know your tribulation and your poverty (but you are rich) and the slander of those who say that they are Jews and are not, but are a synagogue of Satan. Do not fear what you are about to suffer. Behold, the devil is about to throw some of you into prison, that you may be tested, and for ten days you will have tribulation. Be faithful unto death, and I will give you the crown of life.

"He who has an ear, let him hear what the Spirit says to the churches. The one who conquers will not be hurt by the second death."

REVELATION 2:8-11

CHAPTER THREE

PASTORS SUFFER

J esus' life was one of suffering and tribulation from the first day. His words to the pastor of Smyrna, "I know your tribulation and your poverty ... and the slander," are filled with the experience of one who endured in deeper fashion the same afflictions (Rev 2:9). Apparently, a helpless baby born in an inconsequential town amid the squalor of a feeding trough was a large enough threat to the regional monarch that he had to send an assassination squad to end the boy's life. When Jesus' parents were alerted to the danger, they fled the country. As a result, he was a forced refugee immigrant living in a foreign country until all was safe.

His upbringing required fidelity to both God and parent as he had to thread the needle of imperfect parental leadership coupled with knowing and obeying the will of his perfect heavenly Father. Before he could even get his public ministry off the ground, he faced the fiery trial of the devil's temptations during a forty-day stint in the wilderness. Every day with twelve bullheaded and insubordinate young men would be a forced trial in faithfulness and compassion. His endearment of himself to one who would betray him and even more so to one who would deny him was relationship tribulation. The pain of those betrayals and denials may have hurt more than Roman nails in his hands or a crown of thorns on his head.

When brought up to the hour of his crucifixion, he faced the incredible agony of trial by silence. Did his Father not hear his prayers to take the cup of suffering from him? Was his Father unmoved, having no pity for his eternal Son, who was about to lay down his life for the rebel scum of humanity that desecrated the glory and majesty of his name?

He faced the crucible of an unjust trial, a passive and capitulating ruler concerned only for his own political ends, and a crowd determined to see a guilty man go free while an innocent man died. His physical suffering involved the worst of the worst. No form of human torture and execution was designed to be so intimidating, humiliating, and excruciating that the word itself elicits pain. Rome dominated the scene of tribulation through crucifixion. Jesus felt the abandonment of his Father, his disciples, and his people. Even criminals reviled him. He knows the pastor's experience of tribulation.

When it came to wealth and poverty, Jesus was honest when he said he had no place to lay his head (Luke 9:58). He left his eternal glory to live hand to mouth, dependent on the supply of others. Born into a poor peasant household, he didn't have the privilege of a prestigious education at the best schools with promising career advancement. Vocationally, at best he would be a working-class carpenter. Food, bed, rest, even his taxes had to be supplied by others. "Though he was rich, yet for your sake he became poor" (2 Cor 8:9). In death, he hung on a cross of wood naked and exposed. His body's resting place wasn't even his own. Instead of being discarded in the common grave outside the city, a rich man's generosity supplied an unused tomb. The constant affliction of poverty was Jesus' everyday plight. Likewise, he knows the pastor's suffering in poverty.

The reality of being slandered (or blasphemed) is well within his domain of experience as well. He was slandered by his friends, slandered by his enemies, even slandered by his own people. He grew up and ministered under suspicion of being a bastard son. When it came time to discredit his work, the specter of illegitimacy was the card his enemies played against him (John 8:41). He knows what it is to have friends stab him in the back (or worse, kiss him on the cheek). He overheard his closest friend tell strangers, "I do not know the man" (Matt 26:72). He endured religious leaders taking his words out of context, misrepresenting the facts, even making up stuff he never said at all to advance their own agenda. He had to listen to the mockery of those same devils as they verbally assaulted him on the cross saying, "He saved others; he can't save himself" (Matt 27:42). To this day, wicked deeds done in the name of Jesus loudly blaspheme and lie about his character.

The entire scope of suffering contained in tribulation, poverty, and slander are realized in Jesus—which makes him alone competent to stand in solidarity with pastors in our suffering. Or, as the writer of Hebrews put it, "Because he himself has suffered when tempted, he is able to help those who are being tempted" (Heb 2:18).

JESUS, THE FIRST AND LAST IN SUFFERING

The second letter Jesus sends to pastors doesn't go to a leader that has abandoned the gospel, or one who is caught in immoral behavior. This little postcard of fewer than one hundred words comes to a pastor facing the temptations that suffering draws out of us. On those darks days when an email comes with harsh words that have nothing to do with the work we've done, or when we watch another person we've loved willfully destroy every relationship around them—including with us—we are tempted to doubt our calling, or despair over the progress of our work. It even produces a temptation to change our perspectives and practices on what faithful and holy ministry truly is.

The afflictions of pastoral ministry make us wonder if we are actually doing it right. Our aversion to suffering makes us want to fix the source of the pain or, as best we can, avoid it altogether. Suffering disorients us in our faith. Doubts creep in. Questions are raised. We wonder where God is, why he is allowing this to happen, and why he won't smite our foes. Does Jesus really love us when we and our families face the emotional, mental, financial, and relational blows of hatred and abuse that come with being a pastor? David's cry, "How long, O LORD? Will you forget me forever? How long will you hide your face from me?" (Ps 13:1), becomes our own cry.

I wrote this chapter during Holy Week, having just come out of one of the most difficult seasons of my pastoral life. Our church was not immune from the severe polarization borne out of the Covid-19 pandemic, the fights over racial inequality, and the political identity upheaval every church in America faced. In my exhaustion, I feel more than ever my absolute need for Jesus. I see more than ever that pastors need Jesus. The only way we can endure suffering and press on in serving Christ and his church in the midst of hardship is by embracing the man of sorrows who is enough for us. We need a Jesus who is enough for us in the pain of loss, slander, pride, humiliation, fatigue, abandonment, and abuse. We need one who experienced the totality of human suffering and who stands in solidarity with his pastors, ready to strengthen us with all that he is. The suffering Savior shows us he is more than enough.

Do you see how deeply Jesus shows solidarity with us? As theologically trained, biblically literate pastors, we cognitively know Jesus sympathizes with us, as humans *and* as pastors, in our sufferings. We know we're supposed to *say* Jesus identifies with us. But we quickly forget how "acquainted with grief" he truly was. Often, we reduce Jesus' suffering down to just his final week of passion. We attribute his suffering to the culminating and grandest act of all suffering—the cross—yet we miss the way in which every moment of his human experience was a form of suffering. Not just the grand moments, every moment. This makes him fit to stand in solidarity with us. Jesus' suffering and affliction was comprehensive, an experience of suffering in totality.

When Jesus discloses himself to the pastor of the church in Smyrna, he reveals himself as the one who is first and last. I'm quick to want to put a period there, as if this is some theoretical exercise of doctrine with "first and last" declaring his comprehensive deity. Yet Jesus says he is "the first and last, *who died and came to life*" (Rev 2:8). His death and resurrection are immediately and intricately connected to his totality. The opening vision of his nature in Revelation 1 interlocks the same themes. He spoke to John saying, "I am the first and the last, and the living one. I died, and behold I am alive forevermore" (Rev 1:17–18). His comprehensiveness is a comprehension of the totality of suffering. Jesus has more for us than merely an academic or detached understanding of suffering and affliction. He's experienced it. He has suffered. He lived out and experienced suffering from A to Z. He's run the entire gamut of suffering and feels our pain from his very heart.

Which is why he can identify so closely with the pastor who is suffering. To the pastor in Smyrna, and to every pastor under the pain of affliction, loss, persecution, and trial, he says, "I know." He knows it intimately, experientially, comprehensively. Jesus has experienced, in far deeper depths, the sufferings that we all face as pastors. That may be good news for you in the moment you face. The solidarity and sympathy of Jesus is inclined toward you right in the middle of your suffering as a pastor.

Jesus expresses his knowledge of the church of Smyrna's need in three terms. He knows their tribulation, their poverty, and the slander they face. Categorically, it's the shared suffering of his own life as well.

We may be prone to believe that God doesn't see or know our sufferings. Maybe more discouraging would be the thought that he doesn't care about us in those pains. Yet the comprehensive scope of the suffering and trial of Jesus' life is evidence of God's deep care for our sufferings. Jesus is standing in solidarity with his pastors. With you and me in our own sufferings. He stands in solidarity because he *knows* the full range of human affliction and suffering. He *knows* the full experience of pastoral suffering and affliction.

THE FELLOWSHIP OF SUFFERING

When Jesus stands in solidarity with us and our suffering, we don't have merely an empathizer. We don't even have merely a *sympathizer*. Far better, we have a brother. And Jesus is not ashamed to call us brothers and sisters (Heb 2:11). He brings us into a family that shares a distinctive resemblance to one another: the marks of his suffering.

Our union with Christ bears out the encouraging reality that not only does Jesus know our suffering, but our suffering endears us to him. Lest we think our suffering could alienate or drive us away from him, the truth is that our suffering is proof that we actually belong to him. In fact, our suffering is an out-working of our union with Christ. Because pastors belong to Jesus, pastors suffer.

As much as we try to avoid the pain that the curse of sin has brought down on us, the pain still comes. It's as much a part of the pastoral ministry as preaching or praying is. We are told to "share in suffering as a good soldier of Christ Jesus" (2 Tim 2:3). and "do not be ashamed of the testimony about our Lord, nor of me his prisoner, but share in suffering for the gospel by the power of God" (2 Tim 1:8). Suffering for the pastor is a normative reality of ministry. And it's a shared reality. It's a family story.

The vantage point that looking back on history gives us reveals a rich tapestry of fellow sufferers in the gospel. The annals of church history tell story after story of pastors who didn't fare well in their churches and ministries but were inflicted with the pain and torment of various and sundry afflictions. John Calvin faced horrible physical maladies including kidney stones and hemor-rhoids so intense that they sidelined him from ministry altogether. "Much of his study and writing was done while bedridden. In the final few years of his life, he had to be carried to work."[12] Jonathan Edwards was fired from his Northampton congregation over a dispute about who could receive the Lord's Supper. John Bunyan was put in jail for preaching Christ without a license. Athanasius "was accused of murder, illegal taxation, sorcery, and treason—the last of which led Constantine to exile him to Trier."[13] These are just a few of those more well-known pastors who faced affliction and suffering with the church, often at the hands of the church herself, for the sake of the gospel.

Smyrna had her own suffering pastors as well. Within eighty years of Jesus' letter to the pastor of Smyrna, the forewarned tribulation would come. Although John probably didn't know, the blow would fall on a dear disciple and friend of the apostle John, Polycarp. The story recounted tells of a pastor who had been faithful to the gospel in a city hostile to the message of Jesus.

The city was a prominent and prosperous center in Asia Minor. The beauty, wealth, and prestige of Smyrna put them in constant contention with other cities to be known as the "First City" in the region.[14] Smyrna was very religious too, in both a political and nationalistic way, giving itself to the worship of the Caesars. The city was filled with temples and altars to various Roman emporers, like Tiberius and Hadrian, and so Rome responded by bestowing on Smyrna the honorable title of "Temple Warden."[15] The Christians in the city faced a strong "Caesar-only" influence from their neighbors. Added to that trouble was the notorious "synagogue of Satan" that Jesus refers to in his letter (Rev 2:9). Smyrna was home to a significant population of Jews that partnered with Rome in making sure the Christians were not given high standing and influence in the city. Their thirst for blood made them especially dangerous in the community.

This is what brought Polycarp to his end. There was intense pressure to eradicate the Christian "threat" in the city and to make an example out of the church's leaders. In a public spectacle, Polycarp was brought into the stadium to be tried. When he refused to recant Christ or to swear by Caesar, "the whole multitude both of heathen [Roman] and Jews, who dwelt at Smyrna, cried out with uncontrollable fury, and in a loud voice, 'This is the teacher of Asia, the father of the Christians, and the overthrower of our gods, he who has been teaching many not to sacrifice, or to worship the gods.'"[16] Their charge was simply Polycarp's faithfulness to gospel ministry. And it cost him his life. He was tied to a stake to be burned to death,[17] and when the fire wouldn't extinguish his life, he was run through with a dagger and bled out, extinguishing the very fire that tried to consume him.[18]

Whether by physical ailments, slanderous members, political stunts, or cultural hostility, the long line of faithful pastors is marked with the affliction of suffering. We are marked with that affliction because it is the very mark that Jesus carried. German Reformer Martin Luther quipped in a sermon, "Where the preaching or the preacher is not persecuted or spoken against it is not the gospel at all and the preacher is not preaching it. The gospel is always persecuted, and the hypocrites murmur against it, but their works are nothing. Direct yourself by that!"[19] The apostle John had heard Jesus say these very words. "Remember the word that I said to you: 'A servant is not greater than his master.' If they persecuted me, they will also persecute you" (John 15:20).

Notice that Jesus doesn't offer this as a hypothetical statement: "Maybe they will persecute you." He defines pastoral realities with suffering and persecution because that was his reality. In my younger days of ministry, the vision of success that was laid before me was the expansive stadium. In the stadium, thousands upon thousands would hear the good news of the gospel and the wind of the Holy Spirit would blow and revival would fall like never before. I was exposed to the models of Billy Graham, Luis Palau, Greg Laurie, and others filling stadiums and looking to see the wind of the Spirit blow. Their model was the standard of success. Yet I wonder if instead of the stadium of success, the stadium of martyrdom is a more accurate template in the Bible for pastoral ministry.

We read Paul's words in Romans 8:35–39 as a triumphant victory cry over our lives. Who shall separate us from God's love? *Nothing!* But the triumphant victory cry is captured in the context of suffering and tribulation. It's the whole point for the pastor. Who shall separate us? *Tribulation? Distress? Persecution? Famine? Nakedness? Danger? Sword?* Paul speaks of these things as the normative afflictions of the minister. When he quotes the Hebrew Scriptures to land his point, he pulls Psalm 44:22: "For your sake we are being killed all the day long; we are regarded as sheep to be slaughtered" (Rom 8:36). Suffering is entrenched in the very nature of overcoming and victory. The posture of a pastor is that of a sheep being led to the slaughter.

Paul even goes toe-to-toe with the "super-apostles" who were waylaying the church in Corinth by laying out his sufferings as evidence of his being a better servant of Christ than they were. "Are they servants of Christ? I am a better one ... with far greater labors, far more imprisonments, with countless beatings, and often near death" (2 Cor 11:23). I don't know about you, pastor, but I don't have imprisonments, beatings, and being near death as accomplishments on my résumé. But there are sufferings on my résumé (and yours) that are unique to us, which Paul *did not* have.

Because we belong to Jesus, and he is our brother, we join in the fellowship of suffering. We're not alone in our afflictions. They are normative for the pastoral role and serve as identifying markers of our belonging to Christ. Without the stripes we must wonder if we share the Savior.

WALKING IN THE WAYS OF
THE SUFFERING SAVIOR

If this is true—because pastors belong to Jesus, they suffer—then how do we make our way forward in this affliction and hardship we've been called to? What is the family way forward?

Jesus' letter to the pastor and church in Smyrna is exceptionally tender. There is no rebuke, not a list of "five ways to fix your leadership style so the culture likes you." Jesus doesn't offer a leadership coaching session on how to grow your influence and make friends with opponents bent on burning you at the stake. Jesus gives two directives of encouragement that help us navigate how to walk with him in the way of suffering: do not fear, and be faithful.

DO NOT FEAR

When we are about to face hardship or trial, fear is the singular trigger that drives us to change course. Some fears are well-founded and good. Running away because you're walking down a dark street while someone threatens you with violence is a healthy response to fear. Changing your doctrinal statement or failing to preach the whole counsel of God because you fear the response of the world (or a few vocal members) is not a positive response to fear. Fear can help us, but it can also hinder us.

It is this second type of fear that Jesus speaks against. He tells the pastor and church in Smyrna not to fear what they are about to suffer. Fear here for the church in the midst of her sufferings would not be good. How can a person *not* fear knowing that suffering will be coming? Wouldn't all of us fear being thrown in prison? Wouldn't we lie awake at night if we were told we might lose everything; our families might be thrown out on the street, our children starved, and our wives abused? I'd be freaking out!

You would be too *if* you had been drawn into a world of ministry where suffering was abnormal and suboptimal. The twentieth and early twenty-first centuries haven't thrown a lot of daggers at the church in America. There has a been a relative peace between the winds of the world and the ways of the church in the United States. Like the proverbial frog in the pot of water with its subtle rise in temperature, we've been lulled to sleep against the promise of affliction and suffering for Jesus' pastors.

But suffering *is* the norm for the people and pastors of God. So when Jesus says, "Don't be afraid" we have to think about what he means for us to not live in fear of the very things that are fearful to us. Scripture is clear: "All who desire to live a godly life in Christ Jesus will be persecuted" (2 Tim 3:12). If we take it as a fixed reality that because pastors belong to Jesus they will suffer, then when that moment of suffering does fall on us, or the anticipation of the trial looms large in our mind, we can face particular suffering without fear.

Pastors today need a more robust theology of suffering within our daily lives. It's normal that the gospel message will receive an apathetic and hostile audience. It's normal that the trends of culture will blow away from supporting the church and toward opposition to the exclusive claim of Jesus as the only way, truth, and life. It's normal on occasion that members of our churches won't love every word we preach from the Word and in their own hardness of heart will snip and snipe at the shepherd. It's normal that pastors will lose status and reputation in the culture. We'll be considered pariahs and unworthy of trust.

A robust theology of suffering will acquaint us with the man of sorrows who calls us to deny ourselves, bear our cross, and come and follow him. Instead of parading around the country with prestige and popularity (a theology of glory), the pastor should take up a theology of the cross.

Jesus walked through suffering, not in fear, but in confidence that this was his Father's will for him. He endured the trials of betrayal, abandonment, mockery, physical affliction, and even death "for the joy that was set before him" (Heb 12:2). Jesus didn't respond to these tribulations in fear, but with faith in the "definite plan and foreknowledge of God" (Acts 2:23).

Pastor, walking in the ways of your Savior is to take hold of him, not fear, alongside the absolute reality that you will suffer. Our loving and faithful Savior has marked out a measure of affliction and suffering for each of us from his sovereign hand. Do not be surprised that this suffering will come. Do not be afraid when it does.

BE FAITHFUL

The temptation that suffering brings to our lives and ministries is compromise. We believe the affliction we are facing is the result of a mistake or an error or a fault in what we've done. Somehow our mental math told us that if we do all the right things we will ascend the ladder of glory one step at a time. If we fail or falter in some way and experience hardship and difficulty, we didn't do it right. Yet we forget that Jesus himself was perfect in every work of his ministry, and still, as the Apostles' Creed confesses, he "was crucified, dead, and buried. He descended into hell."

The self-help gospel (which is damnable heresy) promises pastors "ten tricks to being as successful as I am." When we have attempted the ten tricks and don't succeed, we pivot to find another method. When the devil slings his fiery darts and arrows at our lives and our churches, we'd like to extinguish those flames with the waters of compromise.

The sad fact is that compromise comes too easy for us. We don't have the stomach to endure too much affliction or suffering. The result is a church shifting from the clear and solid ground of the Scriptures. When attendance or giving drops, we are tempted to modify our message to make sure we don't lose more attenders or see our influence diminished.

Jesus' second tender word to the pastor and church of Smyrna is a call to be faithful, even to death. He tells them to stay the course, don't compromise, don't abandon the faith that was delivered to them. His encouragement is to keep going until you die for his sake, no matter what the city and the culture throw at us. Being faithful doesn't exclusively mean dying a martyr's death for the sake of the gospel. Faithfulness for the pastor of Smyrna, and every pastor since then, is a faithfulness to Jesus that encompasses every area of our lives.

Paul in his second letter to Timothy encourages the younger pastor to entrust what he has been given "to faithful men, who will be able to teach others also" (2 Tim 2:2). Alongside this, Paul adds another command: "Share in suffering as a good soldier of Christ Jesus" (2 Tim 2:3). He then describes faithfulness using the metaphors of a soldier, an athlete, and a farmer. Specifically, Timothy is to ponder the single-minded service of the soldier, the integrity of the victorious athlete, and the diligence of the harvesting farmer. For the pastor this means keeping our eyes on pleasing Jesus, doing our work the right way, seeing things through to the very end. It is, to borrow Eugene Peterson's famous title, "a long obedience in the same direction."[20]

Jesus displayed this faithfulness by walking through suffering even unto death by refusing to compromise. He wouldn't take the devil's offers of the easy way out to gain what was truly offered to him. He wouldn't take an easier road or a more comfortable path to secure his glory. No, he "for the joy that was set before him endured the cross, despising the shame, and is seated at the right hand of the throne of God" (Heb 12:2). Jesus lived as the perfect faithful man by his fidelity to his Father's will, his obedience to and fulfillment of the law in every point, and his suffering unto death.

We can walk with Jesus in our suffering, even to death, as well. Because we belong to him, we can endure the crushing forces of our culture that want to see the church compromise. We can be faithful to preaching Christ and him crucified, even if we lose market share and monetary security. We can be faithful to Christ in all things ethical and doctrinal because we belong to him. It may cost us our lives, but in the words of missionary Jim Elliot, who was faithful to death, "he is no fool who gives what he cannot keep, to gain what he cannot lose."[21]

CROWNS FOR CONQUERORS

Suffering for the sake of Christ is never without reward. Jesus suffered and is exalted. His pastors are encouranged to endure suffering with the promise of an exaltation as well. Just as he humbled himself "by becoming obedient to the point of death, even death on a cross," she he was exalted and given "the name that is above every name" (Phil 2:8–9). Just as pastors are called to "share in suffering for the gospel by the power of God" (2 Tim 1:8), so they will be given "the crown of righteousness, which the Lord, the righteous judge, will award" (2 Tim 4:8).

Jesus offers the same to the suffering pastor of Smyrna, and to all pastors who labor in the affliction of ministry. Jesus promises those who are faithful that they will be rewarded with the crown of life. Even death won't be able to steal away the reward of faithfulness. The crown *is* life.

Is this our desire?

Jesus invites us to listen. The promise is for you and me as much as it was for Smyrna and her pastor. "Let anyone who has ears to hear listen to what the Spirit says." Is the temptation today for you to compromise or cut corners in your ministerial calling? Being tempted to walk away because of suffering, are you ready to abandon faithfulness to Christ? Don't miss what the Spirit says.

For those who conquer, those who stand in Christ, the second death of eternal separation from God won't touch them. In fact, it's an impossibility that the second death would even be a reality for those who belong to Jesus. Jesus has defeated death. He stands over the corpse of death, his spoken word bringing the deathblow to death for us. Those who belong to Christ will never taste the horror of eternal death. Suffering is just a light and momentary affliction not worth being compared to the eternal weight of glory waiting for us.

If you're looking for one to sympathize with your pain, Jesus is enough.

If you're looking for one who's been there and knows the depths of your agony, Jesus is enough.

If you wonder where relief and aid and respite will come from, Jesus is enough.

If you're looking for someone to be nearer to you than a brother, Jesus is enough. ✗

Pastor, in your suffering, abandonment, meager pay, long nights, frustrating board meetings, angry-member emails, frustrating staff departures, misrepresented statements, interrupted family vacations, lost sleep, and all the whirlwinds of trial and tribulation that a local pastor feels, Jesus is enough for you.

He is enough because all his trials were for the purpose of reconciling you to him.

He is enough because all his poverty was to make you rich.

He is enough because all the blasphemy against his name was to give you a new name.

He endured it all so that all who believe on him would have God as their Father, and Jesus as our brother.

He endured it all so that we would forever belong to him.

AND TO THE angel of the church in Pergamum write: "The words of him who has the sharp two-edged sword.

"I know where you dwell, where Satan's throne is. Yet you hold fast my name, and you did not deny my faith even in the days of Antipas my faithful witness, who was killed among you, where Satan dwells. But I have a few things against you: you have some there who hold the teaching of Balaam, who taught Balak to put a stumbling block before the sons of Israel, so that they might eat food sacrificed to idols and practice sexual immorality. So also you have some who hold the teaching of the Nicolaitans. Therefore repent. If not, I will come to you soon and war against them with the sword of my mouth.

"He who has an ear, let him hear what the Spirit says to the churches. To the one who conquers I will give some of the hidden manna, and I will give him a white stone, with a new name written on the stone that no one knows except the one who receives it."

REVELATION 2:12–17

CHAPTER FOUR

PASTORS TEACH AND TELL THE TRUTH

Nearly three decades ago, Eugene Peterson wrote what is now a famous shot across the bow concerning the pastoral vocation, which stunned me when I first read it: "American pastors are abandoning their posts, left and right, and at an alarming rate. They are not leaving their churches and getting other jobs. Congregations still pay their salaries. Their names remain on the church stationery and they continue to appear in pulpits on Sundays. But they are abandoning their posts, their *calling*. They have gone whoring after other gods. What they do with their time under the guise of pastoral ministry hasn't the remotest connection with what the church's pastors have done for most of twenty centuries."[22] *working the Angles*

For years I grappled with the question of what a pastor does. As a baby-faced graduate from four years of Bible college with a bachelor's degree in pastoral studies, I had little idea of what pastoring would actually be like in the local church. I had some experience in internships, but those were merely functional. Do the stuff the youth pastor doesn't want to do so he can do the stuff he does want to do.

When I actually came into my first foray of pastoral ministry, I was eager yet green. I quickly discovered that what was called "pastoring" looked very different from what I had envisioned. Our church was still meeting in a local high school. Pastoring meant being at the building early to set up chairs and stage equipment and tables. As we launched our student ministry to teens, I found we needed to find teens to be able to minister to. Pastoring meant event organizing, promotional work, building a hype factor, organizing the logistics of pizza delivery and cleanup from the inevitable mess that would ensue from a crowd of hormone-driven teenagers. Because I was the only other pastor on staff, there were other areas beyond student ministry I was forced to give oversight to. Pastoring meant organizational meetings, recruiting volunteers, writing policy manuals, evaluating curriculum for kids' ministries, managing budgets for several departments, and even securing supplies for any particular Sunday morning's needs.

Reading Peterson's indictment hit home. Was this what pastoral ministry was supposed to be? Did I dedicate my life to logistics, organizational management, marketing and promotion? Had I misunderstood the calling? Did I somehow sleep through the class on "pastoring as CEO" while in ministry preparation? Was I the recipient of a message that was intended for someone else when I left Moody Church in Chicago one February evening after hearing James Montgomery Boice preach Romans 11:33–36 and sensed the Lord saying, "That's what I want you to do with your life"? "Pastoring" looked and felt very little like what the Bible called us to do.

I became aware of that discrepancy because something deeply fundamental and focal was missing. Peterson illuminates the problem as a shift in what is primary for the pastor. As he put it, "The pastors of America have metamorphosed into a company of shopkeepers, and the shops they keep are churches. They are preoccupied with shopkeeper's concerns—how to keep the customers happy, how to lure customers away from competitors down the street, how to package the goods so that the customers will lay out more money."[23]

Pastors and churches have abdicated their God-given calling and work. The essential job of a pastor has been transformed from one noble and glorious thing to a much less important other thing. Like Martha trading the one thing necessary by being "distracted with much serving" (Luke 10:38–42), so have we as pastors neglected our Christ-given responsibility to the church. Peterson's words poignantly defined for me the pastor's responsibility: "to keep the community attentive to God."[24]

Few I know would disagree with that sentiment. But the means by which we do that work would be up for debate in many circles. How does a pastor labor to bring and keep a community and congregation into attentiveness with God?

I don't think Paul's exhortations to Timothy were throwaway lines in his second letter to the young pastor: "Do your best to present yourself to God as one approved, a worker who has no need to be ashamed, rightly handling the word of truth" (2 Tim 2:15). Or, "All Scripture is breathed out by God and profitable for teaching, for reproof, for correction, and for training in righteousness, that the man of God may be complete, equipped for every good work" (2 Tim 3:16–17). Followed by the charge, "In the presence of God and of Christ Jesus, who is to judge the living and the dead, and by his appearing and his kingdom: preach the word; be ready in season and out of season; reprove, rebuke, and exhort, with complete patience and teaching" (2 Tim 4:1–2).

The template the apostles gave to the office of the pastorate was to "devote ourselves to prayer and to the ministry of the word" (Acts 6:4). The pastoral calling is first and foremost a responsibility before God to minister the Word of God, proclaiming the gospel of Christ as ambassadors and heralds of the King of kings. As J. C. Ryle comments, "We cannot doubt that St. Paul's conception of the minister's office included the administration of the sacraments, and the doing all other things needful for the edifying of the body of Christ. But … it is evident that the leading idea continually before his mind was, that the chief business of a minister of the New Testament is to be a preacher, an evangelist, God's ambassador, God's messenger, and the proclaimer of God's good news to a fallen world."[25]

Where confusion or disorientation about the pastoral office and calling exists, I'm confident it is because we have redefined or abdicated our work as mediators of the Word of God. Our insecurity in being ministers of the Word is a worry that teaching and telling the truth of God in this culture will result in our being refused by the very people we're trying to reach. Acceptance and belonging will be evasive to us if we spend too much time saying what God says.

Our failure here is a failure to see and represent the one we truly belong to. We fail to see our position in Christ and out of our belonging to him uphold and carry out the primary task of pastoral ministry we've been given to carry out. Pastor, because we belong to Jesus, we teach and tell the truth. We deal in the Word of God. We serve to "preach Christ crucified" (1 Cor 1:23) and have been called to be a "minister according to the stewardship from God ... to make the word of God fully known" (Col 1:25). Negligence to our calling as heralds of God's Word puts us in the same predicament in which the pastor of the church in Pergamum found himself. We may even find ourselves on the wrong side of Jesus' two-edged sword.

WHAT THE WORD IS

When Jesus writes to the pastor in Pergamum, he reveals himself by his authority. He opens this letter by declaring himself as the one "who has the sharp two-edged sword" (Rev 2:12). This harkens back to the all-encompassing vision of Christ himself in Revelation 1:16, in which John saw coming from Christ's mouth "a sharp two-edged sword." The symbol is not mysterious. Jesus' word, his speech, is this sword.

The sword was a powerful symbol and countercultural representation of where true authority and power was located. Jesus specifically uses the image of a Thracian broadsword (in contrast to the more frequently referenced "dagger" or "sword" mentioned throughout the New Testament). His choice of this type of sword is to counter the Roman *ius gladii*, or "right of the sword," by which sovereign authority and power were meted out. "Here it is probably used because the Roman proconsul in charge of the province resided in Pergamum, and the symbol of his total sovereignty over every area of life, especially to execute enemies of the state, ... was the sword."[26]

Instead, Jesus reveals himself to his pastor as the ultimate sovereign who has the right of the sword. In Abraham Kuyper's words, "There is not a square inch in the whole domain of our human existence over which Christ, who is Sovereign over *all*, does not cry: 'Mine!'"[27] Jesus alone possesses all authority in heaven and earth (Matt 28:18), and he wields his authority through his word. What Jesus says is true, right, good, perfect, and powerful. Jesus "upholds the universe by the word of his power" (Heb 1:3).

Before Jesus ever has anything to say about the Pergamum problem and the pastor's ministry there, he positions himself in opposition to the cultural perspective of where true power and authority really lie. The pastor of Pergamum needed to know and believe that Jesus held a higher power and authority than the most powerful of powers in his city, the Roman proconsul.

We too need to understand the nature of Jesus and his authority. Our cultural climate is quick to dismiss any base or structure of authority over our autonomy and independence. We're told to live our own truth, craft our own identity, do whatever we want, be whatever we desire, live however we desire to write the script. Any attempt to exert authority over us is met with disdain and rebellion. We are to be tolerant and accepting of everyone and everything no matter what. That tolerance is only given as long as you affirm the particular "truths" of everyone everywhere. Make any claim to a singular and absolute truth and you'll be met with the canceling fury of the highest degree. The threat of being labeled as a bigot, intolerant, or nonaffirming and being canceled in the community today is a powerful right of the sword that culture holds over our heads.

But Jesus' right and authority is far greater. When we get down to the necessary nature of pastoring as the ministry of the Word, we find ourselves at a crossroads. We either take up pleasing God in the stewardship of the Word, or we bend to pleasing people and tremble underneath the tyranny of slavery to the whims of the world. Paul makes the distinction clear for us: "For am I now trying to persuade people, or God? Or am I striving to please people? If I were still trying to please people, I would not be a servant of Christ" (Gal 1:10 CSB). We're either ministering his Word as servants, or we're out there working to please people.

Because the Word of God is the power of God for salvation, because it is the inspired and God-breathed means by which Christ rules and reigns over all the universe, and because Christ himself identifies his word as the double-edged blade, "piercing to the division of soul and of spirit, of joints and of marrow, and discerning the thoughts and intentions of the heart" (Heb 4:12), we best not diminish, sideline, or compromise on the priority of the ministry of the Word in our congregations. Jesus, the Word of God, has called us to speak his Word, feed his flock, call his own, and "proclaim the excellencies of him who called" us "out of darkness into his marvelous light" (1 Pet 2:9). Jesus, with his sovereign and absolute word, rules, reigns, creates, and sustains all things.

When we take stock of the one who has the sharp two-edged sword and realize his supreme authority and relevance in the universe, we can be assured we have all we need to fulfill our responsibility to "keep the community attentive to God" even when the cost may be high in our culture.

As Jesus addresses the pastor in Pergamum, he is supporting and supplying him with the essential and primary means of ministering in a culturally hostile climate. Jesus entrusts the pastor the "right of the sword" through the Word of God, and if the pastor will wield the Word of God rightly, he will have enough to stay faithful, holy, and true.

PASTORING WITH THE WORD
TO STAY FAITHFUL

Jesus' knowledge and love of the church and its pastors come to every context and situation. It isn't a surprise for the Word of God to be aware of the hostile evironment and high stakes of living in the crooked and oppressive world. In five of the seven letters, Jesus begins the body of the letter by declaring his knowledge of that pastor's works. He knows what the pastor is doing and what the ministry has accomplished. In the letter to the pastor in Smyrna, he spoke of his knowledge of his suffering and poverty. Here in the letter to the pastor of Pergamum, he does not address actions or afflictions; he identifies the address: "I know where you dwell" (Rev 2:13).

This understanding of where the pastor lives comes with a more disheartening description: "I know where you dwell, where

Satan's throne is." This pastor wasn't just ministering in a secular culture, he was ministering at the very epicenter of evil. By God's calling on his life, he went as far frontline as he could and approached the very gates of hell to make the gospel call to sinners in need of rescue. He was pastoring where the lies would be loudest, most seductive, and more believable than ever before.

Pastoring in Pergamum was a constant battle for truth. The city's prominence in Asia Minor was a result of their political clout, the seat of Roman power in Asia Minor. With a population estimated at over 150,000 in the first century, Pliny called the city the "most famous place of Asia."[28] But it wasn't just a political capital. Religion itself was big business in Pergamum as well. Within the city, temples stood to just about every Greek and Egyptian deity one could think of: Athena and Zeus holding the most prominent places. Many believe the prominent altar of Zeus was what Jesus was referring to when he mentioned "Satan's throne." "Pergamum would indeed have seemed to him a stronghold of Satan, perhaps the location of his very seat of power as he deceived humanity to take what was due God and give it instead to sticks and stones and pretentious human rulers."[29]

Even though "Satan's throne" was just down the street from the pastor and his church, Jesus commends him: "Yet you hold fast my name, and you did not deny my faith even in the days of Antipas my faithful witness, who was killed among you, where Satan dwells" (Rev 2:13). My imagination is filled with curiosity about this event, of which we have only this record. Apparently the pressure and conflict were so great that one of the first true martyrs for the faith came out of the city of Pergamum. The enemy was so hostile and the lies were so great that they resorted to violence to ultimately kill a member of the congregation who would not bow down to the idols of the city. The right of the sword dished out by Roman leaders ready to assert their dominance may have had the first word, but they won't have the last.

We would be wise to ask what helped Antipas stay faithful. What gave him the courage to endure suffering and give up his life when the offer to recant and live came up? Beyond Antipas, Jesus is commending the pastor and the church. If we as pastors saw one of our congregants executed horrifically—some church history legends in later centuries suggest Antipas was boiled alive—what would sustain us to stay the course and not give in or recant ourselves? If we fear people and believe the right of the sword belongs ultimately with those in power here and now, we'll be easily tempted to abandon the faith ourselves.

Yet when we hold fast to the Word of God, we are equipped to sustain suffering and tribulation. Endurance grows out of hearing and receiving the Word of God. Paul's direct counsel to Timothy gave reality and perspective to suffering and persecution. In calling Timothy to recall "my teaching, my conduct, my aim in life, my faith, my patience, my love, my steadfastness, my persecutions and sufferings that happened to me" (2 Tim 3:10–11), he was calling Timothy to faithfulness in light of suffering because "all who desire to live a godly life in Christ Jesus will be persecuted" (2 Tim 3:12). He could admonish Timothy to, "continue in what you have learned and have firmly believed, knowing from whom you learned it and how from childhood you have been acquainted with the sacred writings, which are able to make you wise for salvation through faith in Christ Jesus" (2 Tim 3:14–15).

By pastoring with the Word, you equip and enable your people to keep the faith. The regular and consistent preaching of the Word of God is a call into the shaken and stirred lives of God's people to believe the truth and abandon the lies of where our security ultimately is found. Those who uphold and give high esteem to the Word of God over the church equip God's people to endure suffering, calamity, and all sorts of pressures that would cause our brothers and sisters to shipwreck their faith.

Over the years I've discerned a telltale sign that people are about to do serious damage to their faith. I don't always see it immediately, but when it is noticeable, I become worried. Every person I've counseled who has "deconstructed" their faith, or frankly just walked away from Christ altogether, has done so by starting with abandoning the Word of God. They quit regularly attending and participating in regular worship services and hearing the gospel Word proclaimed. They abandon spiritual community with other believers who listen and apply the Word of God to their daily lives. They isolate themselves from other Christians and start to doubt or deny the trustworthiness and authority of Scripture. It's been my experience that folks will depart from churches with a high view of the authority of Scripture to congregations that treat the Bible more like a fortune cookie with pithy sayings. Before too long they have left the faith altogether. But it all begins with an abandonment of God's holy Word.

When pastors give priority and prominence to the ministry of the Word in their congregations, they are pointing to the ultimate power and authority of Jesus, who is the very one who keeps us. They are wielding the Word of God to fulfill Jesus' promise, "Truly, truly, I say to you, if anyone keeps my word, he will never see death" (John 8:51).

PASTORING WITH THE
WORD TO STAY HOLY

As we wield the Word of God within our churches, we not only supply them with the Spirit-given means to remain faithful but also apply the means of grace for their holiness.

Of great importance to Jesus is the sanctification of his bride, the church. He cleanses her "by the washing of water with the word, so that he might present the church to himself in splendor, without spot or wrinkle or any such thing, that she might be holy and without blemish" (Eph 5:26–27). The ministry of the Word of God within the church is the means by which the people of God are purified and made more like Christ. Unfortunately, this was where the pastor in Pergamum was failing in his responsibility. Some in the church were not attentive to God because they were buying the lies and falsehood of heretical teaching, which led to heretical living.

Jesus turns to address a branch of false teaching that was gaining greater and greater influence in the church herself. He makes a comparison of the false teaching in Pergamum to a parallel situation from the Old Testament. Specifically Jesus identifies the misguided gentile prophet Balaam, who influenced Israel to syncretize their worship through eating to the god Baal and committing sexual immorality with the Moabites (Num 25:1–3; 31:16). In the same way that Balaam influenced or "taught" the people of God that it was appropriate and permissible to worship Baal and engage in the sex acts of the cult of Baal, so some in the Pergamum congregation were teaching that joining in the temple worship of the Roman deities and the acts of sexual immorality were right and permissible.

Within the church in Pergamum, as with the church today, the need for holiness is great. There are far too many ways in which our churches match our culture. We are called to be set apart for Christ, and to live lives of distinctive ethical purity. It is therefore distressing that *within* the church, teachers are leading astray the flock of God in regard to holiness. We may have churches that are robust with the strongest and clearest theology, but there is no doubt that true practical holiness is in short supply. The ethics of Christ's call to sacrificially love our neighbors is traded for "owning" our political enemies. Our speech is as toxic and vile as the world's. We weaponize our words to destroy the opposition. We love money more than anything; greed festers in our congregations.

Jesus' call to repentance for the pastor is to step into his primary responsibility as a minister of the Word. By laboring to teach and tell the truth, the pastor calls the church to holiness. When he leads in preaching the Word, he engages the church to listen to Christ himself and "put away all filthiness and rampant wickedness and receive with meekness the implanted word, which is able to save your souls" (Jas 1:21). He serves like Jesus by taking the Word of God and washing the feet of his disciples who need to be cleansed (John 13:8). He commands the blessing of Psalm 119 for the one who keeps "his testimonies, who seek him with their whole heart, who also do no wrong, but walk in his ways!" (Ps 119:2–3).

One of the greatest joys I've had in ministry is to see people grow in holiness because they have heard the Word of God, received it, and walked in obedience to the Lord. I've seen it happen at different times and in different settings, not just from the pulpit, but it always encourages me that God's people are becoming more and more holy through their exposure and reception to God's Word. In a sermon series on 2 Corinthians 8–9, many shared with me how they were formed in their understanding and practice of giving specifically to the poor because what they heard from the Word. On several occasions in premarital counseling sessions, unmarried couples who were sexually active and cohabitating received the pure milk of the Word and practiced chastity before their wedding date. When I've taught on passages like Ephesians 2 on the gospel as God's work to reconcile us to himself *and* to one another, I've borne witness to members of the church repenting and repairing the broken and estranged relationships they had with other brothers and sisters in Christ.

Jesus' work to purify and cleanse his bride always comes through the heralding and teaching of his Word. Pastoral ministry is more than just preaching and teaching the Word of God, but it is never less than the preaching and teaching of God's Word. The very means God has ordained for holiness in the church is the tried-and-true way for pastors to minister effectively. If we would see our people grow in holiness, we must wield the Word of God.

PASTORING WITH THE WORD TO STAY TRUE

The trouble with teaching and telling the truth today (as it has been all along) is that when we affirm one thing, we are also likely denying another. If I were to say, "The sky is blue," I would also be denying any claims that the sky was green. By our affirmations and denials, we find ourselves in agreement or disagreement with others. Lines are drawn, fences are built, and tribes are assembled. These divides are not necessarily evil or wrong. I for one would not want to be in the tribe that stood at the top of the Grand Canyon and declared, "Gravity is a myth." The problem for us is that by our affirmations and denials we find ourselves "in" with some and "out" with others. If the others have something we believe would make our tribe better (for instance, power, influence, wealth, approval), we find ourselves on the horns of a dilemma trying to either gain the others' acceptance or take from them, even by violence, the desired gain.

This dynamic is what motivates so many pastors in their ministry today. Our truth claims affirm and deny certain realities in the world, and that puts us "out" with the culture. Yet we want the approval, acceptance, prestige, or even the peace of not being harassed for our beliefs that the world offers. So, what happens to the truth? We hide it, downplay it, or even deny it in order to cross the line of being "out" and enjoy the sense of belonging.

When Jesus corrected the pastor of Pergamum for his allowance of false teaching in the church, this fear of not belonging was likely a motivator that invited him to tolerate an abandonment of the truth. By permitting some to "hold the teaching of the Nicolaitans" (Rev 2:15) in the church, this pastor was exchanging the belonging he had in Christ for the affirmation and belonging he could have in the community itself. By failing to "keep a close watch on [himself] and on the teaching" he was jeopardizing the truth he was committed to uphold (1 Tim 4:16).

While there is some question regarding what the Nicolaitans taught, it is clear that the teaching was a deviation from the gospel. Jesus' encouragement to the Ephesian church was that they "hate the works of the Nicolaitans, which I also hate" (Rev 2:6). Yet here in Pergamum, Jesus says, the teaching and works of the Nicolaitans are affirmed and practiced. These teachings, as best as we can reconstruct, were syncretistic practices to retain place and power in the community. These teachers, within the church herself, were telling believers "there was nothing wrong with participating in the imperial cult, since even most Romans did it out of civic duty rather than actual worship."[30] The festivals to Caesar, they reasoned, were just patriotic gatherings, not worship services. Yet the events at the festivals were a betrayal of the truth of God's Word. "Both eating meat offered to idols and [sexual] immorality were in direct contradiction to the Apostolic Decree, which forbids gentiles to practice either (Acts 15:20, 28–29; 21:25)."[31] Truth was sacrificed for acceptance and belonging.

Pastoring as a minister of the Word of God is fundamentally dealing with truth and error. It is always an affirmation of what is true from God's Word and a correcting and disciplining away from the errors and lies that Satan, our sin, and the world throw our way. When we lead as pastors with the Word of God, we serve God's people by bringing them onto the straight paths of life. When we neglect our responsibility to proclaim the whole counsel of God, we leave God's people susceptible to the "fierce wolves" of false teachers who will not spare the flock (Acts 20:27–29).

One of the major concerns of almost every New Testament epistle is with false teaching in the church. One of the essential requirements for a person to serve in the office of pastor is that "as God's steward ... he must hold firm to the trustworthy word as taught, so that he may be able to give instruction in sound doctrine and also to rebuke those who contradict it" (Titus 1:7, 9). That is to say, Jesus has given the responsibility of teaching and telling the truth to pastors. Not only has he given us the responsibility, but he's also given us the means to carry out this calling—his Word! "Sanctify them in the truth; your word is truth" (John 17:17).

When pastors fail to uphold this responsibility, they can be sure they will find themselves on the wrong side of Jesus' "right of the sword." He tells the pastor in Pergamum to repent of his passivity in refuting the false teachers. Repenting means wielding the truth, correcting the falsehood, bringing God's truth to his people so that they will walk in the light and enjoy the truth. Repenting means preaching the Word "in season and out of season"; reproving, rebuking, and exhorting "with complete patience and teaching" (2 Tim 4:2). If we don't care enough for Jesus' flock by teaching and telling the truth, we can be sure Jesus himself will come and wage war "with the sword of my mouth" (Rev 2:16). He is the Truth. He won't tolerate his flock to be deceived into error and falsehood by a negligent pastor who is fearful of proclaiming, "Thus says the Lord!"

FEASTING ON THE WORD

Pastors, we must consider the nature of our calling. What is our stewardship and responsibility to Jesus and his church? "Let anyone who has ears to hear listen to what the Spirit says."

We are to be wielders of the Word, stewards of the supremely authoritative "word above all earthly powers." We need to take hold of Jesus' promises to pastors who are faithful in teaching and telling the truth. It's a promise of eternal belonging and fellowship in God's new community.

If fear of being excluded, ostracized, and even penalized by the Roman authorities and powers of Pergamum kept the pastor from wielding the Word of God faithfully, then only a superior promise of belonging would encourage him to uphold his calling. Jesus offers all this to the one who overcomes.

Instead of a compromising feast with the food sacrificed to the idols of Rome, Jesus offers "some of the hidden manna." He replaces the food that defiles with the bread of life that comes from heaven. Instead of a ticket for admission into the parties and orgies that signaled who was "in" around Pergamum, Jesus gives "a white stone" as a token of induction into his heavenly banquet and eternal feast. Jesus replaces earthly approval that came at the cost of denying the truth with eternal fellowship that only comes from holding fast his Word. Instead of a popular reputation and name in the community, Jesus offers "a new name written on the stone that no one knows except the one who receives it" (Rev 2:17). Jesus replaces the fleeting praise of people with the glory of belonging to God. "The nations shall see your righteousness, and all the kings your glory, and you shall be called by a new name that the mouth of the LORD will give. You shall be a crown of beauty in the hand of the LORD, and a royal diadem in the hand of your God. ... And as the bridegroom rejoices over the bride, so shall your God rejoice over you" (Isa 62:2–3, 5).

The promise here is an invitation to feast on and enjoy forever the fellowship and intimacy of the Word of God. Jesus, as the Word of God, gives himself as "the bread that comes down from heaven, so that one may eat of it and not die" (John 6:50). We, as ministers of the Word, are promised to have all that Satan offers but cannot deliver as we hold fast to the truth. Our calling is to preach Christ, to feed on his flesh and blood by faith, to partake of the living Word of God.

Jesus, the Word of God, is enough for us to teach and tell the truth. May we pray with Martin Luther as we serve as ministers of the Word:

> Lord God, You have placed me in your church as over-seer and pastor. You see how unfit I am to administer this great and difficult office. Had I previously been without help from you, I would have ruined everything long ago. Therefore I call upon you. I gladly offer my mouth and heart to your service. I would teach the people and I myself would continue to learn. To this end I shall meditate diligently on your Word. Use me, dear Lord, as your instrument. Only do not forsake me; for if I were to continue alone, I would quickly ruin everything. Amen.[32]

AND TO THE angel of the church in Thyatira write: "The words of the Son of God, who has eyes like a flame of fire, and whose feet are like burnished bronze.

"I know your works, your love and faith and service and patient endurance, and that your latter works exceed the first. But I have this against you, that you tolerate that woman Jezebel, who calls herself a prophetess and is teaching and seducing my servants to practice sexual immorality and to eat food sacrificed to idols.

"I gave her time to repent, but she refuses to repent of her sexual immorality. Behold, I will throw her onto a sickbed, and those who commit adultery with her I will throw into great tribulation, unless they repent of her works, and I will strike her children dead. And all the churches will know that I am he who searches mind and heart, and I will give to each of you according to your works. But to the rest of you in Thyatira, who do not hold this teaching, who have not learned what some call the deep things of Satan, to you I say, I do not lay on you any other burden. Only hold fast what you have until I come.

"The one who conquers and who keeps my works until the end, to him I will give authority over the nations, and he will rule them with a rod of iron, as when earthen pots are broken in pieces, even as I myself have received authority from my Father. And I will give him the morning star. He who has an ear, let him hear what the Spirit says to the churches."

REVELATION 2:18-29

CHAPTER FIVE

PASTORS BECOME LIKE JESUS

No one ever stepped into pastoral ministry in order to have a moral failure. I can't think of one prominent former pastor, or even a lesser known one, who would say, "I went to seminary thinking I'd give this a run for a decade or so then crash the ship and run off with another person in my church." Yet it seems as if moral failure is becoming a common theme among Christian leaders today. It's not a matter of *if* you will fall and disqualify yourself from leadership in the church. It seems to be a question of *when*. Almost every month I hear of more leaders who have disqualified themselves from serving because of a moral failure. Many of those failures are sexual. A transference has occurred; pastors have made the ministry about themselves. The anecdotal trends seem to display a trajectory: the higher a pastor rises in popularity and mass appeal, the more likely his fall will be. My network of pastors often laments these falls and moral failures. Articles appear with titles like "Ten Signs You're Headed for Moral Failure." We read postmortem tales of what should have been done to prevent the collapse. We all do a lot of proverbial navel-gazing. We want to be sure it doesn't happen to us, as if we are passive victims to the whims of the Moral-Collapse Monster.

We don't enter this vocation to fail. But so many do.

We can sit and blame the pressures of ministry. After all, pastoring is working in the pit. We have the busyness of preaching each Sunday, leadership meetings, emails to answer, couples to counsel, sick to visit, staff to develop, Bible studies to teach. Each week the pressure mounts to keep all these things afloat. When the offerings aren't as much as needed, or the conflict in the church is greater than could be expected, or merely the exhaustion of one more need hitting your desk, it can be easy to collapse. Pastors turn to binge eating, drinking, pornography, and many other excesses to defuse the pressure. Escapism becomes a method of flight from the pressure of ministry. Little compromises are taken. Self-justifications are made to validate a guilty pleasure. A feeling of entitlement is fostered. Slowly, step-by-step, a pastor becomes what he never intended to be.

Sometimes it's the systems of accountability (or lack of accountability) that are faulted. The pastor wasn't surrounded by the right people. He wasn't asked the right questions. He was such a winsome leader that any kind of moral ineptitude was unfathomable to consider. He was trusted too much. Critics were envious of his position and status; they just wanted to take him down. The list could go on.

Regardless of whether a pastor's fall is accounted for by the pressures placed on him or the failure of the systems surrounding him, the summary is always the same. Sin has disqualified the leader from further ministry and brought shame and disgrace on the church herself. A pastor always has to make sure that he lives "above reproach" before the Lord and before the world so that he might keep his reputation unvarnished, and his ministry accomplishments secured.

I remember sitting in a breakout session at a high-profile pastors' conference hearing a prominent college and young-adults pastor speak about living above reproach. He said the main reason he sought to be a man of integrity and moral excellence was because he never wanted to face the day when he would have to come home to his wife and children and tell them of his failure. He didn't want his years of laboring in ministry and his ministry's growth to be all for nothing. At the end of the day, he wanted the legacy of his work to last far beyond him.

As noble as this sounds, I had to wonder—is the goal of personal holiness and moral integrity in pastoral work just keeping up an impeccable reputation? I wonder if a subtle shift has occurred in our motivations about why we pursue righteousness and live lives of consistent godliness and holiness. Could it be in our language about these motivations that we are still putting the spotlight on our own work, our own successes, and our own reputations? We (maybe as subtle narcissists) don't want our track record to be discredited, or shame brought down on our name, or worst of all, to go out as a moral failure. Instead, we live by a code that ensures that our reputation will be as unblemished as possible on the last day.

I suspect this shift has occurred because pastors have traded their secure belonging in Christ for the alternative yet elusive security of building something that endures. We are achievers. We want our work to have a lasting impact and lasting fruit. Most of my Bible-college peers who were aiming for missions ministry or pastoral appointments, myself included, were in it with the ambition to do something that stands for eternity. We had the gauntlet of Jesus' parable of the faithful servant thrust before us. Leaders would tell us, "Don't be the foolish or unwise servant who didn't return a profit on the gifts he had been given. Be sure to labor hard so that you hear the longed-for words of God about your work, 'Well done good and faithful servant.'" (see Matt 25:21, 23). It astounds me that so many pastors, who are faithful, godly leaders, are filled with anxiety, wondering if they've done enough to hear those words.

So we live in fear. We are constantly anxious, hoping that we're doing enough and being enough, and making sure there aren't any perceivable flaws around us so that we have a reputation and legacy that last through the annals of history. Our sleepless nights are filled with the trembling fear that we aren't doing enough or that we'll be discovered for the frauds we actually might be. We have to keep up a reputation. We have to project successes and wins. We're constantly working to keep an impeccable look and hide all the ugly stuff backstage. Ministry is all about doing the right things in order to secure the right reputation we all want to be known for.

Except something is missing. Actually, some*one* is missing: Jesus.

THE PROTECTING, PROJECTING PASTOR

Jesus doesn't seem to be concerned with keeping up a reputation. Maybe that's because there is absolutely *zero* threat to his eternal glory and status. He has been given the name that is above every name (Phil 2:9). His kingdom is an everlasting kingdom that will never be destroyed (Dan 7:14). He is so secure in his position, authority, glory, and status that he truly is the "non-anxious presence" when it comes to building a reputation and preserving a name for himself.[33]

Even the way he identifies himself in the letter to the pastor of Thyatira reveals a secured self-awareness. He *is* "the Son of God" (Rev 2:18). No doubt remains over his identity. With "eyes like a flame of fire," the risen and vindicated Son of God looks with piercing insight and clarity into the milieu of this church. He stands before them with "feet ... like burnished bronze," demonstrating unmovable power and stability. There is nothing about Jesus here that comes across as if he is insecure, anxious, or threatened by the disarray within the church of Thyatira. His ultimate glory isn't threatened, even if his church and the pastoral leadership of that church are neck deep in tarnishing the reputation of Jesus, the Son of God.

There is a strange discrepancy within the pastor and church in Thyatira. On the one hand, Jesus commends this pastor for his "works, your love and faith and service and patient endurance, and that your latter works exceed the first" (Rev 2:19). Isn't that all any pastor and church would want said for them by the Son of God? If we're looking for a description of success in ministry, this has to be one of the very best. There is a clear trajectory of growth in the categories that are most essential in pastoral ministry. Pastorally speaking, the work of the ministry—preaching, prayer, administering the sacraments, and the like—are known. The love this pastor has for Jesus and his congregation is abundant and evident. No person is turned away. When it comes to dependence on the Lord and trust in him, he gets the highest marks. Even the way this pastor serves the poor, needy, and outcast receives approval. When it comes to dealing with the pressures and trials of his cultural context, this pastor again receives Jesus' approval. Jesus has seen this pastor grow and grow and grow.

Yet there is a major moral problem within the church. This pastor has been faithful and successful in so many of the right categories, but he has succumbed to a pressing threat within the very church herself. The dissonance of the situation is troubling. Jesus pulls the curtain and reveals a gross moral mess in the midst of *his* church. He uses the strongest language and monikers to identify how repulsive their sin is. By invoking the name Jezebel, Jesus recalls the wife of Israel's king Ahab, who "incited" her husband to give himself above and beyond any other "to do what is evil in the sight of the Lord" (1 Kgs 21:25–26). By her influence, Israel dove deep into idol worship that was filled with sexual immorality and debauchery. It was the same kind of practice happening in the merchant city of Thyatira, whose economic well-being came from the prominent trade guilds that served as the social glue of the city itself. Gordon Fee remarks, "Each of these guilds had their patron deities, and the primary social events among the guilds were the festive meals, where food was served in a context of where it had been sacrificed to the patron deity. Very often these meals became an occasion for sexual immorality to flourish, where 'girls' were made available at the male-only meals."[34]

Just like Jezebel, a prominent person in the church was teaching and encouraging the church to follow her lead and ignore this clear violation of the holy conduct God's people were to embody. This "threat-level Jezebel" teaching and immorality was going unchecked. Like the rapid advance of stage-four cancer, her teaching and conduct spread around the congregation and the impending judgment was promised to be devastating. Jesus declares that unless they repent the fallout will be so catastrophic that "I will strike her children dead. And *all* the churches will know that I am he who searches mind and heart, and I will give to each of you according to your works" (Rev 2:23). Jesus is clearly saying he will make an example of them.

The discrepancy of this pastor's life raises a big question. How can a pastor be so highly commended on one hand and yet tolerate such deplorable evil within his ministry on the other? Yes, it is true that the church is *simul iusta et peccatrix*, at the same time justified and sinful. The reality is that each of our lives, and the collective lives of the church together, is a spectrum of greater and lesser degrees of holiness. We're a mixed bag, and if a church is true to its mission then it should be a place where sinners are received and given space to hear Jesus' gospel word and be loved by a congregation dedicated to Jesus. But that isn't the issue for the pastor of Thyatira.

I believe that what paralyzed this pastor and prevented him from addressing the false teaching in Thyatira, and letting it go unchecked for an unknown amount of time, was fear. At some point early on, when the false teacher began seducing and leading the church astray, the pastor was filled with fear and sat paralyzed, refusing to act because of what he believed the issue meant about him. He was afraid of the stain on his darling reputation as a pastor and leader. It was easier to ignore and dismiss the issue altogether rather than address this spiritual wolf head on, lest people leave the church. If people brought it up as a concern in the church, he could just point to all the things Jesus would commend: "But look at all the fruit! Can't you see how good things are going here?" He had a reputation to keep and a status to attain.

I know this fear and paralysis all too well.

Every year during my annual review with my church leadership, I wrestle with my own sense of approval, acceptance, and significance. During one particular review, my insecurities all boiled to the surface. The year prior our church had had a relatively informal system for reviewing campus pastors. We were asked to rate ourselves on certain competencies and goals, and then went through a document that contained our campus "vitals" (things like baptisms, new members, average Sunday-morning attendance, engagement in small groups, Bible studies, and our finances). I was affirmed and celebrated and told, "You are a model of what we want a campus pastor to be at Woodside." I loved hearing that affirmation. I worked hard for it.

The next year, however, was different. A new formalized system was put in place. New ratings, standards, processes for the review were defined. I plunged ahead using the prior year's scoring rubric to rate myself on my competencies and goals with an assessment of our campus vitals. As you can guess, I gave myself very high marks. I was after all a "model campus pastor."

Nothing but disgust and despair came when the report was returned back to me with instructions to fill it out again. I was told I had rated myself too highly. I wasn't Jesus! I was told to try again and give myself more accurate and moderate ratings on par with the rest of the leadership at Woodside. I fumed around the house after reading the email, probably barking at the kids for no good reason. Looking for an ounce of sympathy and solidary in the face of this injustice, I shared the audacious email with my wife, Stephanie. I received no sympathy for my tantrum.

Instead, she lovingly put her finger right on the issue. "Jeremy, they are right. I mean, you gave our marriage health the highest rating you could, but we have work to do. Bring your scores down to earth." She pointed out what I didn't want to acknowledge: I was a model campus pastor—but I had work to do. My projected reputation *and* the reality of having sin to deal with and weaknesses in my ministry work were in direct conflict. I would have rather ignored my weaknesses and failures and instead broadcast all the things I was doing right. If my failures were pointed out, I knew I'd never belong to the Pastoral Hall of Fame.

BELONGING TO THE HALL

My theological tribe has a fascination with church history. Maybe rightly *and* wrongly so. We are indebted to the work of the Reformers and look at them as heroes. Luther, Calvin, Knox, and others stand tall in our gaze for their preaching, teaching, and work to clarify the gospel, purify the church, and get the Bible into the hands of ordinary people. Their titanic battles against popes, kings, and heretics are the stuff we nerd out on. And we believe that perhaps we can have a similar reputation ourselves. My tribe (what was once called the Young, Restless, Reformed movement, although by now we are all middle-aged) doesn't want to be forgotten generations from now. We're working as if we'll be seen as the next Luther or Calvin. Some of us are hoping our books will be bestsellers one hundred years from now (present company included). We're preoccupied with building something that will last.

We want to be known as the generation that held the line, even reformed and purified the church, just like our spiritual forefathers did. While there are pure and good motives for this, one of the main motives that lies under the covers of our hearts is that we want people to be impressed with us. Future generations, we hope, will acknowledge that we held the line and even turned back the tides of secularism, legalism, and watered-down attractional-based ministry, or any other threat we choose to identify.

We build (or plant) so that we will belong.

But we're not hoping to belong to any one person. We want to belong to an elite club. We want to belong to a Hall of Fame. We want to be named in history! And we haven't forgotten the adage: those who win write history. So we want to win; we want our names to go down in the stories of the victors. We want to belong to that elite club in heaven that only Calvin, Luther, Huss, Edwards, Sproul, and Augustine will enter. I'll say it again: we believe our building (or planting) of churches, ministries, and ultimately our reputations is a means of securing a belonging.

Perhaps you think I'm overgeneralizing. You don't really want to be in *that* club *that* badly. Maybe not. But how would you know? The discordant reality of a pastor who is strongly affirmed for his ministry and yet ignores deep flaws internally tells us that the issue of Thyatira is our issue. Instead of looking at Thyatira's problems as if through a window, the story of the pastor in Thyatira needs to be turned into a mirror for us to reflect on ourselves.[35] We need to see the signs that could tell us we are building and protecting a reputation in order to belong. Jesus' rebuke of the church, and directly of this pastor, helps us see three characteristics that show we are focused on and motivated by establishing and protecting a ministry reputation.

MISTAKEN IDENTITY

First, the leaders in Thyatira had an identity problem. More specifically, they were using titles to inflate their identity, instead of pursing who they truly were.

The ringleader of the group that was entrenched in sexual immorality and debauchery had taken up a title for herself. Jesus exposes it by saying she "calls herself a prophetess" (Rev 2:20). It's almost mockery on Jesus' part: "*She* calls herself ... [but I don't]."[36] The title was self-assumed, self-appointed, self-aggrandizing. In order to lead a following, she had to have some clout. To give validity to her flagrant rebellion, she took on a title endued with authority, prominence, and spiritual power. Even the title of "prophetess" was an act of seduction and deception on her part. While pastors, deacons, and even deaconesses were part of the common leadership of a church, to have a prophetess show up would be a spectacle. Her perceived spiritual authority would be seen as more exciting and alluring than just the normal pastor who preached and administered the sacraments each weekend. This case of delusional identity paved the way for her to "teach and seduce" people into her immorality.

It happens today all the same. When leaders stand on titles, whether real or contrived, they position themselves as builders and movement-makers. The title becomes the identity and core reality of the person. If our identity is staked on the positions we hold and the titles we bear, we are dangerously putting the spotlight on ourselves. If we demand that others call us by our titles or revere us because of them, we are in danger. If brothers and sisters cannot approach us, even to lovingly help correct us, because we are "Most Revered Doctor Pastor," it is evident that we are building and protecting a reputation that results in our induction the Hall of Fame. When we use members of our staff and volunteers in the church to defend or shield us because of our titles, we have overemphasized an identity in ministry. If we deflect rightful correction and concern with the excuse, "I'm the pastor and you don't touch God's anointed," we show a heart that is anchored to a reputation.

This isn't to say our titles aren't important. The office of pastor and elder carries a high calling, and dignity, respect, and reverence for those who hold the office should be shown. This is why the writer of Hebrews follows his statement about the responsibility of the overseer with a directive to the church at large: "Obey your leaders and submit to them, for they are keeping watch over your souls. ... Let them do this with joy and not with groaning, for that would be of no advantage to you" (Heb 13:17). As a pastor you are entrusted with a sacred office. But it is a perversion of the gospel and our calling to turn our office into an identity.

TOLERANCE OF SIN

Second, there was a clear toleration of sin *in* the church. Jesus flat out critiques the pastor as the primary one responsible for dealing with the false teacher and her sin. The verb here is singular and direct: "you tolerate" (Rev 2:20). One lexicon says the term has the sense of leaving "it to someone to do something, with the implication of distancing oneself from the event."[37] It's not your problem, not your issue, not your responsibility, not your place. The pastor abdicated his role in "keeping watch over [his] souls, as those who will have to give an account" (Heb 13:17). It's easier to run programs, develop courses, administrate events, even stand on a platform and preach each week than it is to chase after the sheep that is wandering from the fold.

Furthermore, when you get into the work of involving yourself in someone's life and having to call to repentance those who are stuck in their rebellion, the results may not be favorable. A relationship is always on the line when you have to tell someone they are wrong. The closer the relationship, the harder it is to expose that sin and call for repentance in our friends. Even though we have a greater relationship and stewardship to Christ, we tend to weigh more heavily our human relationships and therefore pass on making any kind of disruptive noise. Many pastors refuse to get too close to people in their churches for this very reason. They will have to point out error, call it sin, and then take the pain of a strained and even lost relationship. The failure to act boils down to a fear of man.

Another reason we tolerate sin is because we feel inadequate to really deal with it ourselves. We know that we have our own logs in the eye and that trying to remove the specks in our brothers' and sisters' eyes feels hypocritical. We want to move slowly, at the "speed of grace." The truth is, we never move at all. Fundamentally, we are revealing a deficient view of sin itself. Our doctrine of the pervasiveness and comprehensiveness of sin needs to be better informed. It's not grace to leave untouched sin in our own lives, and especially in the lives of those we are called to minister to. We don't fear God rightly when we fail to deal with the sin that is inhabiting and infesting our congregations, even though we are deeply aware that we also are sinners.

Shouldn't we look within and ask ourselves why we don't address immorality when we see it? Could it be that one reason we aren't dealing with immorality in our ministries is because we would have to acknowledge our ministry isn't as impeccable as we'd like to think? Maybe we believe we have to keep the ministry, or "the brand" (as some have given themselves to calling it), as pristine as possible. Our default approach to hearing about immorality in the church, especially in leadership, is to suppress the information. We're just like our first parents, off and hiding in the bushes so that no one sees our vulnerabilities. Our pride kicks in to protect our cathedral of prominence.

REFUSAL TO REPENT

The saddest characteristic of a reputation-maintaining, legacy-building heart is the stubborn refusal to repent. We see Jesus' constant grace and affection for the soundness and spiritual health of his people in his patience. How difficult are the words, "I gave her time to repent, but she refuses" (Rev 2:21). In the King James Version Jesus says, "I gave her space to repent." She had plenty of room to acknowledge her rebellion. There was room for her to come into the light and come clean with her immorality and to receive the restorative grace of God. No one is too far gone, in this life, to be out of the reach of the grace of God.

However, when we are building ministry monuments to ourselves, any kind of tarnish on the edifice detracts from our glory. Instead, we excuse ourselves and decide not to acknowledge that it's a thing at all.

When I think about the pastoral scandals that have rocked the church in the last decade, including those on a national scale and those on a more local scale, one common trait stands out: damning defensiveness of the integrity of the leader. Instead of acknowledgment, humility, and repentance, what abounds is defensiveness, justification, gaslighting, and brash arrogance resulting in refusal to own up to one's sin. All this in an effort to protect their reputation, secure the brand and legacy, and pass blame on to victims who would "be responsible for millions of souls lost when [their] reputation was damaged."[38]

When the goal is to be in the Hall of Fame for what you have done in ministry, you will do everything you can to protect yourself. Gratefully, Jesus tears down these kinds of efforts. He promised staggering discipline of the cohort that was leading the church in Thyatira into spiritual apostasy, and he will rip asunder anything that stands in the way of his universal glory and triumph. Jesus won't compete with the little monument to yourself called "your ministry" that you spent twenty-five years building.

CHANGING THE GOAL: FROM BELONGING TO BECOMING

If we are so busy projecting and protecting our reputations in ministry in order to be inducted into a nonexistent Pastoral Hall of Fame, what happens when we open up about our faults? If we get real and honest about our weaknesses, if we pull our heads up out of the sand and begin to address real issues in the lives of our congregations, what would happen? If we were to start dealing with the deadly sins that kill churches and bring shame to the name of Jesus, starting with our own sins and failures, could anything good come of it?

As pastors, we want to build good reputations for ourselves, for the church, and for Christ. We want to be able to look back and hear not just from God but also from our churches and our communities, "Well done!" But we often want that word spoken to us as an affirmation of what *we* did, rather than an approval of what Jesus has done.

When we build from an effort to belong, especially to the elite A-Team, Pastoral Hall of Fame club, we end up building fortresses to protect ourselves and reputations from any deficiency, blight, or accusation that could be raised against us. We project and protect in order to earn a place of approval for ourselves.

Instead, what if we remembered that we *already* belong? There is no Hall of Fame. There is a King and his kingdom, and we cannot get any more into it than God's children already are.

I'm hopeful our theology is robust enough for us to affirm that we believe our salvation is the work of Jesus alone on our behalf. We contribute nothing to our salvation apart from the sin that we need saving from. Jesus in his perfect obedience, his sacrificial atonement, his glorious resurrection and triumphant vindication has alone won our salvation. All we do is throw ourselves in faith on his work and believe his promise that "everyone who calls on the name of the Lord will be saved" (Rom 10:13). As pastors immersed in the gospel, we know this old path well. What we tend to forget is the nuances of what that "salvation" means. Certainly, it includes salvation from hell, salvation from sin, salvation from death. But it's also a salvation *to* something. Our salvation is a gift of beautiful spiritual blessings that are just as much gifts of grace, earned by the work of Christ, as our redemption is. This includes the reality of God's pleasure with us.

Instead of attempting to earn our acceptance through the projection and protection of our reputations, what if we realized that we are already accepted fully and completely by Jesus? The doctrine of justification by faith alone in Christ alone isn't just a legal doctrine that lets us rest at night because we are declared "not guilty." It's a doctrine that frees us to venture out in life and grow to become more and more like Jesus *because* we are in Christ. That is to say, I can pursue holiness as the goal of my life and go through all the ups and downs and failures and temptations and setbacks of still being a sinner knowing that I am justified and accepted already and completely because of what Jesus has done and my union with him. I can get up off the mat when my sin knocks me to the ground and go another round seeking to be more like Jesus because I am already righteous before the Father. I can "preach, die, and be forgotten"[39] because the goal isn't to get into the Hall of Fame. It's to be like Christ.

I say all this to pivot our goals away from earning a spot in the Hall and the belonging that goes with it and to point our goals toward who we are becoming. Because we are justified and united with Christ, we already belong. Now it's time for us to talk about who we are becoming. Or to put it this way: because pastors belong to Jesus, they become like Jesus. We are to "grow up in every way into him who is the head, into Christ" (Eph 4:15). Yes, we pastors are to equip the saints for the work of ministry, but we are also called to be "growing into maturity with a stature measured by Christ's fullness" (Eph 4:13 CSB). We don't have to build a reputation that gets us into the Hall. We already belong to Jesus, so we can live that way. In Thyatira certain signs revealed the efforts of a pastor to build and protect his reputation so that he could belong. But if we stand on the reality that we belong to Jesus, then a new set of signs display our goal of becoming like Christ.

RECEIVED IDENTITY

The first sign of our becoming like Jesus is a received identity. Thyatira had bought into the false identities of people who were stacking up titles as rungs on a ladder to get to the top. But pastors don't need titles or letters after our names to inflate our credentials or build our reputations. We already have a glorious and eternal identity bestowed on us from God. We are his children. We belong to him!

The sonship we have in Christ legitimatizes and secures us forever. To the pastor who wonders if he will hear "Well done, good and faithful servant," consider when that statement came for Christ. It's essential for us to understand that before Christ did any ministry work in his full humanity, he received full approval from his heavenly Father. At his baptism recorded in Matthew's Gospel, as Jesus came up out of the water, heaven was opened to him, the Spirit descended to rest on him, and the Father said, "This is my beloved Son, with whom I am well pleased" (Matt 3:16–17). Our union with Christ, pictured in our own baptism, is a reminder of our received identity. There we are immersed in "the name of the Father and of the Son and of the Holy Spirit" (Matt 28:19). We are his adopted, beloved sons and daughters. God is well pleased with us!

This received identity frees us up to pursue becoming who we already are. We are liberated to obey the moral commands (imperatives) of the Bible because they are built on the established identities (indicatives) of who we are in Christ. Paul can instruct us to "put to death therefore what is earthly in you: sexual immorality, impurity, passion, evil desire, and covetousness, which is idolatry" (Col 3:5). But this command stands on the received identity of who we are in Christ: "raised with Christ ... Your life is hidden with Christ in God. When Christ who is your life appears, then you also will appear with him in glory" (Col 3:1, 3–4).

The doctrine of justification reminds us that we are declared holy and righteous with the righteousness of Jesus, which we receive by faith. The doctrine of union with Christ tells us that our justification is a gift because of our location in Christ. These two doctrines dance together to give us an identity of right standing and approval with God. They give every pastor who has trusted Christ alone a true identity. I don't have to labor to build an identity of holiness for myself. I already have one because Jesus earned and gifted his righteousness to me, and I am in Christ. I can become who I already am.

HEARING JESUS

The second sign that displays our goal of becoming like Christ is beholding. We become like what we behold. The apostle Paul states, "And we all, with unveiled face, beholding the glory of the Lord, are being transformed into the same image from one degree of glory to another" (2 Cor 3:18). For the pastor to become like Christ, he must behold Christ. How do we behold Jesus? We see him by hearing him. To hear his voice is to see him, because Jesus is present in and through his Word.

We often forget the privilege we have of being in vocational ministry. Part of my job description is to be daily in the Word of God, meditating on the beauty and excellence of Jesus. I am commanded by Scripture to preach "Christ and him crucified" (1 Cor 2:2), which mandates that I take unhurried time to perceive Christ and his atoning work on my behalf. I study the Word seeking to grasp how "every story whispers his name,"[40] and then go and "proclaim the excellencies of him who called you out of darkness into his marvelous light" (1 Pet 2:9). I *get* to do this each week. With Scripture in hand, I am laboring to get fresh views of the glory of Jesus, not just so I have something to say in a sermon or Bible study, but so that *I* am transformed into the glory I am seeing.

Since we belong to Christ, seeing his glory should be the preoccupation of our hearts. Whenever I perform a wedding ceremony, I like to watch the groom's face as his bride walks down the aisle. You can see the twinkle in his eye as he seeks to take all of her beauty in. I often take a longer pause at the beginning of the ceremony just so he can take her in. Because we belong, we too can take the long pause and see Christ. As we do so we will see how amazing he is.

I like to encourage pastors to take time every year and slowly read through one of the Gospels. Get a journal and note to yourself Jesus' character and actions. How does he speak? What does he teach? How does he respond to the circumstances in front of him? What surprises you about Jesus? Taking the time to see Jesus through his Word will develop Christlikeness within you. As you behold Jesus, *hear* Jesus, the Holy Spirit will transform you to become like Jesus.

FAITHFUL OBEDIENCE

The third sign displaying a goal of becoming like Christ is that we step out to walk with Jesus in obedience to him. Receiving our identity from Jesus and hearing Jesus regularly strengthens us to walk with Jesus in every situation. Here's where the action is for us, but notice, it's all built on Jesus' action first. As we watch and listen to Jesus, we begin to participate in the walk of life he lays before us.

Pastors must pursue holiness. It's essential to our continued qualification and authority in ministry: "An overseer must be above reproach" (1 Tim 3:2). We must be careful to walk a "long obedience in the same direction"[41] and discipline ourselves, "lest after preaching to others I myself should be disqualified" (1 Cor 9:27). Holiness is paramount to the pastoral calling.

This holiness is, as Harold Senkbeil puts it, "participating in the presence of God yet today"[42] or, "baptismal therapy: the death of the old Adam and the resurrection of the new man."[43] This participation in the presence of God includes repenting of our sin and believing the gospel daily. It includes going to war against our sinful nature (mortification) and to "be killing sin or it will be killing you."[44] The pursuit of Christlikeness is a pursuit of putting on the thoughts, affections, behaviors, speech, emotions, and life of Christ. We start striving to become like Jesus because we are in Jesus, we hear Jesus, and are with Jesus.

BE THE CONQUEROR YOU ARE

When you and I realize that we already have the approval and divine pleasure of God, then pastoring to belong is honestly silly. We already belong, and now we can become who we are. In

Christ we are already conquerors. Now we get to grow up into the conquerors we already are.

Not everyone in Thyatira had succumbed to the false prophetess's seductions. They weren't paralyzed by the same fear that kept their pastor from addressing the idolatry and immorality that was festering in the congregation. They were just trying to be faithful to Jesus. What does Jesus say to them in the midst of a church replete with moral compromise and idolatry? More directives? More laws? No. He gently tells them, "I do not lay on you any other burden. Only hold fast what you have until I come" (Rev 2:24–25).

Jesus' promise to the "one who conquers" is a powerful tonic for the fearful pastor who is worried about protecting a reputation and yet realizes there is work to do. Jesus knows this even in the way he shares the promise: to "the one who conquers *and* who keeps my works until the end" (Rev 2:26). Both belonging and becoming are brought into the picture. Because he is in Christ, the pastor of Thyatira is a conqueror; there is no reputation to protect. Yet because he belongs to Christ, he has work to do. He can deal with the sins of immorality in his life and church.

The nature of the promise shows us just what growing up into Jesus means for us on that last day. The language here is taken straight from Psalm 2. Just as Jesus bears the title "Son of God," ("The LORD said to me, 'You are my Son' " [v. 7]), so we are gifted the title of adopted sons and daughters of God. Just as Jesus rules the nations as his inheritance and with his authority, so he gifts to his pastors authority and power over the very cultures that sought to subdue and dominate them. "The basis of our participation in the messianic victory is our participation in his messianic power."[45]

Furthermore, the Son of God gifts the overcoming pastor "the morning star" (Rev 2:28). This imagery is used later in Revelation, where Jesus describes himself as "the root and the descendant of David, the bright morning star" (22:16). He gifts to his pastors all that he is and all that he has so that they will become all they were redeemed to be. "He is morning star as Davidic king, so in receiving Jesus the star, the victors are raised to shine like kings in the firmament.[46]"

Pastor, "let anyone who has ears listen to what the Spirit says." I began this chapter recognizing that none of us went into vocational ministry in order to fail. And yet we are surrounded by failures. Our own failures are the most glaring and disappointing. We can pretend they don't exist and somehow keep pointing to the good works we are doing as evidence that we are worthy of belonging. Or we can receive what Jesus has gifted to us in all that he is for us. Will we believe the doctrines of justification by faith and union with Christ are the liberating truths that empower us to continually go to work becoming like Christ because we already belong to him?

Be free from the reputation-keeping, the Hall of Fame-seeking, and the fear-of-man thinking that paralyze you from owning up on the weaknesses and deficiencies of your heart and ministry. Instead stand and gaze on the one whose eyes are like blazing fire and whose feet are burnished bronze, the one to whom you belong, and become more like him.

AND TO THE angel of the church in Sardis write: "The words of him who has the seven spirits of God and the seven stars.

"I know your works. You have the reputation of being alive, but you are dead. Wake up, and strengthen what remains and is about to die, for I have not found your works complete in the sight of my God. Remember, then, what you received and heard. Keep it, and repent. If you will not wake up, I will come like a thief, and you will not know at what hour I will come against you. Yet you have still a few names in Sardis, people who have not soiled their garments, and they will walk with me in white, for they are worthy.

"The one who conquers will be clothed thus in white garments, and I will never blot his name out of the book of life. I will confess his name before my Father and before his angels.

"He who has an ear, let him hear what the Spirit says to the churches."

REVELATION 3:1-6

CHAPTER SIX

PASTORS ABIDE IN JESUS

There is no doubt, the calling of a pastor is high. We are servants of God as ministers of his Word to the people of God. The pastoral office is consumed in laboring for the sake of Jesus' people, the church, to become like Jesus in all things. We're commissioned by God (and our churches) to be servants of God, stewards of the gospel, and shepherds of the flock.

Furthermore, the character a pastor must have to hold the office is equally high. We must be leaders who are "above reproach" (1 Tim 3:2), holding "firm to the trustworthy word as taught" (Titus 1:9). Peter tells pastors they are to "shepherd the flock of God that is among you ... being examples to the flock" (1 Pet 5:2–3). Paul speaks of the character of the pastor as being such that he "set the believers an example in speech, in conduct, in love, in faith, in purity" (1 Tim 4:12). The summary command for the pastor is to "keep a close watch on yourself and on the teaching. Persist in this, for by doing so you will save both yourself and your hearers" (1 Tim 4:16).

Factoring in the high calling and high character required (to say nothing of the high competence in executing our role) may remind you the tension this creates. The pressure to keep the community attentive to God causes us to believe that we always have to be at our best. We tell ourselves that for pastors there can be no bad days, no days in which we let our guard down or show our frailty. We lie to ourselves and believe that as pastors we can't have a bad sermon, or give unhelpful or inadequate counsel. The myth we affirm is that pastoring means we're on call 24 hours a day, 7 days a week, 365 days a year. We believe we must be impeccable in our character and so we have to be evasive and hide even when we fail and walk in sin.

Sadly, believing these lies puts us in a place where we believe we must pretend.

In almost every moral failure of a pastor that I am aware of, there is a common trend of concealment, hiding, and isolation. These leaders had all undertaken to bury their sin. Leaders who were close with the fallen pastor often said in astonishment, "That's not who I knew that person to be." The pastors assumed an alter ego that made them appear one way in the spotlight, and they hid their real selves in the shadows where no one would see or know.

Even those pastors who are not hiding moral failure still wrestle with having to be "on" all the time. We wear a face that keeps our congregations from believing anything is wrong, or that there may be difficulty in our marriages, our homes, our work, even our faith. We put on masks so that our community will think "everything is awesome."

But everything isn't awesome, is it?

We're frail, we're sinners, we're tired, we're lazy, we're (dare I say) average. Pastoring as a high calling for leaders with high character and high competency means we had better be exceptional people. We craft and curate our reputations and personas so that we're always seen in the right light. In order to prove ourselves exceptional, we ramp up what we're doing and our activity. The busier we are, the more exceptional we will appear. We become pastoral workaholics in our efforts to curate an impressive ministry. In our minds we believe that our activity as pastors gives us value. This creates a sinister cycle. We curate an image of exceptionalism, and so we do more, and in doing more, we have to put on more masks of exceptionalism to hide how weary we are, which means we do more to keep up the ruse. I wonder if we have forgotten who we really are under all the masks of respectability and activity. I wonder if, in pretending about who we are and how we are doing, we're also deceiving ourselves.

JESUS IS THE ANSWER

In each letter sent out to the seven pastors, Jesus personalizes a bit of self-disclosure for that community. It should not surprise us that the Great Physician is able to bring specific and particular treatment to the various ailments and spiritual diseases that afflict pastors. He knows his sheep, and he knows exactly what they need to be made whole.

To address the pastor at Sardis, Jesus discloses himself as the one "who has the seven spirits of God and the seven stars" (Rev 3:1). We know these stars to be the leaders or pastors of the churches. Jesus reminds the pastor in Sardis that he holds him. The reason for this reminder is to encourage and secure the pastor in his true identity. In the body of the letter to the pastor in Sardis, Jesus doesn't commend him for anything. Unlike every other church where there is a note of affirmation, whether for their endurance or love or good works, the pastor in Sardis receives no approving comment.

Rather, in trying to help the pastor see correctly who he is, Jesus has to speak directly to the situation. His words will be straightforward and clear. Yes, the pastor is still held in Jesus' hand. The love and kindness of Christ rings out here. "I have you," he says to the pastor playing pretend.

But that's not the only thing he has. Jesus also tells us he has "the seven spirits of God." Consistently throughout the book of Revelation, this description of the "seven spirits" is a reference to the one Holy Spirit in his glorious perfection.[47] Jesus told his disciples that at his request the Father would give them the Holy Spirit (John 14:16). The Spirit would be sent in Jesus' name by the Father for the help and comfort of his people (John 14:26). As Jesus further affirmed, "It is the Spirit who gives life; the flesh is no help at all" (John 6:63). In Jesus saying he has the Spirit, he is remarking on the intimacy and fellowship they eternally share.

I love how Jesus talks about who he is here. I can hear him saying, "Okay pastor, I've got you. I've got the Spirit. Now let's talk about what's really wrong. And while we're talking about it, remember who I am and who I have. The answer to your problems may become clear here shortly. You may figure something out. You may see something (or someone) you've been missing."

REPUTATIONS AND REALITIES

I don't know about you, but I am concerned about what people think about me. I want to be seen fulfilling the standard of the office I carry. I desire to be known as a man of great integrity, skill, wisdom, and impact. The competitive parts of my heart and soul want me to be first among equals when I'm in the room with other pastors. Sometimes, like the regional manager Michael Scott in the television sitcom *The Office*, I want people to be afraid of how much they love me.

In all honesty, I want to have a great reputation.

But I know I'm not perfect. I have weaknesses, blind spots, deficiencies, even sins that don't permit everyone to think highly of me. I've hurt and wronged and failed others in ways that result in their distance and disappointment with me.

On one occasion as a youth pastor, I was called into the senior pastor's office. The prior Sunday I had filled the pulpit for him while he was on vacation. With a head full of knowledge and a heart full of pride, I put the bully in the pulpit and railed against some hobby-horse position that I was so sure our church was compromising on. I received a few anonymous letters from parishioners who were troubled with my sermon. The comments my senior pastor received, however, were not anonymous, and I had made a mess. When challenged about my sermon and my posture, my pastor gently rebuked me, but he laid out the problem very clearly. In my arrogance and youth, I became defensive. I was so sure my position was right, and my sermon was good. I gave every convincing argument I could about why I said nothing wrong and the issue was really the spiritual immaturity of the people who couldn't stomach the truth I was dispensing. I was not going to have a reputation as a compromising, capitulating pastor.

If we're honest, many of us are deeply concerned with our reputations. We're so concerned about our reputations that we make sure we cultivate the best image of ourselves we can muster.

If you were to visit the city of Sardis in the late first century, you'd find a city that was very concerned about its reputation. It had developed a reputation for being a "legendary" city. The legend of King Midas told of him leaving his gold in the springs of the Pactolus River, which ran through the city. But the greater legend of Sardis was its fabled existence as an impregnable city. The fortress of the city was seated high on the cliffs, and if you were to talk about "capturing Sardis" you were saying you could do the impossible.[48]

The pastor's concern over his reputation was part of his dilemma as well. Jesus speaks directly to the pastor about it: "I know your works. You have the reputation of being alive." For this pastor and his church, the desire to be known as a vital and lively church was burning hot in his heart. Yet, like the city's legendary status, the pastor's reputation was a legend as well. Jesus puts things in stark terms: "You have the reputation of being alive, but *you are dead*" (Rev 3:1).

Jesus lays out the problem, and there is only one way to say it: This church that prides herself on looking alive is actually spiritual dead. This pastor who curates an external reputation of activity and success is internally devoid of spiritual life.

Could we be the pastors of Sardis? It's one thing for us to observe Jesus' diagnosis. It's another thing for us to consider his words and ask ourselves if we are liable to the same critique today. Are we spiritually dead and yet pretending as if we're vibrant and alive? How would we know?

I believe the answer to those questions is found in how we answer the question John 15:8 raises. Jesus declared, "By this my Father is glorified, that you bear much fruit and so prove to be my disciples." The question, then, is, How is a pastor fruitful, proving to be his disciple? How do you define fruitfulness or explain where it comes from?

One explanation for us is that fruitfulness is a result of our works. We get to work, put our hand to the plow, become active and busy with ministry. You might call this our activity. This answer is natural to our mechanized, industrialized, technological culture. We conceive of spiritual life the way we conceive of mass producing some appliance or vehicle. This kind of spiritual formation is envisioned as an assembly line, in a linear manner. Converts run the bases and take classes 101, 201, 301, and 401; and at the end of that process the machine has churned out another mature disciple of Jesus. Bearing fruit is a result of our labors. At the center, we produce our life.

The other explanation is counterintuitive to our Western way of thinking. It's an agricultural perspective. Fruitfulness comes from abiding in the source of life. Spiritual vibrancy is not a result of our external exertion and activity, but a byproduct of our remaining connected to and drawing nourishment from the source of life directly. Jesus envisioned this means of formation as abiding in him as a branch abides in a vine: "Abide in me, and I in you. As the branch cannot bear fruit by itself, unless it abides in the vine, neither can you, unless you abide in me. I am the vine; you are the branches. Whoever abides in me and I in him, he it is that bears much fruit, for apart from me you can do nothing" (John 15:4–5).

Life is *given* to us. We are recipients of both vitality and fruitfulness. In fact, true spiritual fruitfulness is the result of spiritual life.

The point here is to draw out where we believe fruitfulness is sourced, because our source reveals our life. If our fruitfulness is sourced in our activity, then we exchange worship of Jesus with worship of ourselves in the name of Jesus. We are dead with a reputation of being alive.

On the other hand, if our fruitfulness is sourced in our union with Christ, then we are recipients of the very life that makes us fruitful. John Kleinig calls this "receptive spirituality": "Our spirituality does not come from having spiritual powers or from our spiritual self-development but depends on our faith in Him. Because we are joined to Christ, we continually receive our life from Him."[49]

To escape the deception of having to be enough or living with a reputation that is more legendary than it is legitimate, Jesus calls pastors to abide in him. And yet, it's the abiding in Jesus that we struggle with. We would rather replace it with activity for Jesus.

AWAKENED BY THE SPIRIT

If the problem of our hearts is a dead spirituality projecting a reputation of life, we need drastic measures. We need a wakeup call. Jesus says precisely this.

To the pastor in Sardis, who thinks he's alive yet is dead, Jesus commands "Wake up" (Rev 3:2)!

To the pastor who is self-promoting and self-projecting, performing and parading so he is noticed and applauded, Jesus commands, "Wake up!"

To the pastor hiding, dodging, and isolating himself so his sin is not revealed, Jesus commands, "Wake up!"

To the pastor tired and weary from overworking, always doing, Jesus commands, "Wake up!"

To the pastor externally fine yet internally dry, Jesus commands, "Wake up!"

To every pastor who belongs to Jesus, he calls us to "wake up!"

His command is a command to call forth faith. Just as "Abraham believed God, and it was counted to him as righteousness" (Rom 4:3), so we are called to believe in the one "who gives life to the dead and calls into existence the things that do not exist" (Rom 4:17). Jesus himself calls us to wake up to the life he gives to his pastors. He is the one who is enough to supply for us the entirety of what we need.

This is where abiding in Christ begins. We must be made alive by the Spirit. Jesus, the one who has his pastors, is the one who has the Spirit. The Father is abundantly ready to "give the Holy Spirit to those who ask" (Luke 11:13). Jesus' word, received with faith, is how we receive the Spirit (Gal 3:2). Jesus declares, "It is the Spirit who gives life; the flesh is no help at all" (John 6:63). For Jesus to call the pastor of Sardis and his church back to life means that he must give them the very Spirit of God, who raises the dead to life again (1 Sam 2:6–7). And Jesus certainly gives his Spirit to his pastors.

When we teach John 15 and Jesus' call to abide in him, we have to pay attention to an important yet often overlooked order that Jesus establishes. Namely, there is an abiding that takes place in the life of a disciple before the disciple is commanded to abide in Christ. We must put John 15 in the context of the entire Farewell Discourse of John 13–17. When Jesus tells his disciples that he is departing (which implies his betrayal, death, resurrection, and ascension), he tells them he is not leaving them alone. "I will not leave you as orphans" (John 14:18). In fact, he promises to give them "another Helper, to be with you forever, even the Spirit of truth" (John 14:16–17). And it is here Jesus tells them where abiding starts; not through a connection they muster up with the divine through an out-of-body state of mind or by legalistic obedience to a list of commands. They have the Helper, the Spirit of truth, *abiding* within them!

Many of our English translations of John 14:17 obscure this reality by saying the Spirit "dwells with you" (ESV) or "lives with you" (NIV). Yet Jesus uses the same word here to describe the Spirit's abiding in the believer as he does in chapter 15 to describe the believer abiding in the vine. All this to say, our abiding in Christ follows the Spirit's abiding in us. Jesus gives us his living, abiding Spirit to make us alive and cause us to remain in Christ. As Andrew of Caesarea, one of the church fathers, explains it, "Both [pastors and the Spirit] are in the hand of Christ, for he governs the former as Lord, and as the *homoousios* [one who is the same substance as the Father] he is the supplier of the Spirit."[50]

Which means this: pastor, you must be made alive by the Spirit. You must be regenerated, or "born again." The Spirit himself is the one who gives life. He does this in his sovereign freedom: "The wind blows where it wishes, and you hear its sound, but you do not know where it comes from or where it goes. So it is with everyone who is born of the Spirit" (John 3:8). Yet that does not put us in competition with others because there is a scarcity of life in the Spirit. He freely gives life to all who will humble themselves and believe the gospel. Being justified by faith in the atoning work of Jesus Christ gives us hope, "and hope does not put us to shame, because God's love has been poured into our hearts through the Holy Spirit who has been given to us" (Rom 5:5).

Jesus' warning that not all those on the last day who stand before him and say "Lord, Lord" will enter the kingdom of heaven is sobering (Matt 7:21–23). Just as there are those who come every Sunday and sit in our Bible studies and participate in the activities of the church yet are not born again, so there are pastors who are not born of the Spirit either. Sure, they may preach fine sermons or be a listening, receptive presence. Having an appearance of godliness, they deny its power (2 Tim 3:5). Charles Spurgeon wrote of such leaders, "Unconverted ministry involves the most unnatural relationships. A graceless pastor is a blind man elected to a professorship of optics, philosophising upon light and vision, discoursing upon and distinguishing to others the nice shades and delicate blendings of the prismatic colours, while he himself is absolutely in the dark!"[51]

Abiding in Christ begins with being enlivened by the Spirit. Our awakening by the Spirit of God is absolutely essential to our call.

THE FRUIT OF ABIDING IN CHRIST

Abiding in Christ begins first and foremost by his awakening and enlivening us by his Spirit. This is essential. But that's not where abiding in Christ starts and stops. Jesus calls us to action. He called the pastor of Sardis to get to work because "I have not found your works complete in the sight of my God" (Rev 3:2). Yet that activity is not what made the pastor and church alive. Their activity was to flow out of their abiding. Or to say it another way, they bore the fruit of faith and obedience as a result of being united to the Spirit of life. "Apart from me you can do nothing" (John 15:5).

Jesus' command to the pastor at Sardis is not given without the enablement and power to carry out that command. Being enlivened by the Spirit of God gives the pastor true spiritual vitality and vigor. Because we are awakened by the Spirit we are also empowered to "strengthen what remains and is about to die" (Rev 3:2). This is no enigmatic statement. In verse 3, Jesus tells us exactly what spiritually enlivened ministry looks like. It is a return to the means by which spiritual life comes, the Word of God.

The command of verse 3 is simple: "Remember, then, what you received and heard. Keep it, and repent" (Rev 3:3). It is this simple work that the pastor must identify, return to, and remain in. As I have said before, the work of the pastor is nothing less than a stewardship of the Word of God. Pastoral ministry isn't rocket science. It is work through the empowerment of the enlivening Spirit of God by the means of the Word of God. We must remember and plant deeply within all our ministry philosophies and strategies the reality that "faith comes from hearing, and hearing through the word of Christ" (Rom 10:17).

To be a pastor is to go back to the gospel again, and again, and again, and again, and again. Paul called the gospel word that he delivered "as of first importance" (1 Cor 15:3). He too had to remind a very active but very spiritually dead church in Corinth "of the gospel I preached to you, which you received, in which you stand, and by which you are being saved, if you hold fast to the word I preached to you" (1 Cor 15:1–2). The Word of God is what the Spirit of God uses to do the work of enlivening and revitalizing what is spiritually dead among us.

Martin Luther, pointing to his own ministry as an example, notes this in a sermon: "Take an example from me. I opposed indulgences and all the papists, but never with force. I taught, preached, and wrote God's word alone; otherwise I did nothing. And while I slept, or drank Wittenberg beer with my friends Philip and Amsdorf, the word did so much that the papacy weakened in such a way that no prince or emporer ever inflicted such damage upon it. *I did nothing; the word did everything.*"[52]

Pastor, be renewed and washed by the cleansing of water with the word (Eph 5:25–27). Let the gospel word work, enlivened by the Holy Spirit, renew and refresh your dry, tired, anxious, striving soul. Instead of putting the pressure on yourself to always be doing, always acting, trust the Lord to accomplish his good and perfect will in the church. Receive the word of God daily in your life. Rest and take a day off. After preaching the gospel word, drink a beer (or whatever other beverage you'd enjoy) with your friends and let the word do the work.

Preach the Word and let the Spirit empower your congregation to do what the Lord has called them to do in their vocations, talents, and giftings to glorify God and build the church; it doesn't have to look like an empire with your name on the billboard. Let go of constantly evaluating your performance based on how many people told you the sermon was good or shared it on Facebook. Turn off your phone, ignore your email, log off of Twitter, and be present with your family. Worship Jesus with humility and gratitude in all things, because you recognize that you can't receive one thing unless it's been given to you from heaven. Smile and serve your congregation even when your attendance figures are down and you're half the size you were a year ago. Rest in the promise of Jesus that he has chosen you and appointed you to go and bear fruit and that the fruit that is born will remain. Jesus will build his church (Matt 16:18)!

The reputations we are trying to cultivate and the wholeness we are pretending to embody can be transformed by the enlivening and empowering Spirit of God through his Word. I don't have to be defensive when someone comes to me with a critique or comment on how I can grow. There is no reputation to uphold or protect, and therefore I can receive these kids of comments with grace. I don't have to put on a mask that makes it appear as if everything is awesome. I can be real and honest with myself and others because I have the Spirit abiding within me. I can lament in my prayers and be honest with God not having to cloak my discouragement. Jesus is the source of life; he gives his pastors exactly what they need.

GLORIOUS GIFTS FOR THE
ABIDING PASTOR

Not all was lost in Sardis. Jesus points out that there are some in the church that "have not soiled their garments, and they will walk with me in white, for they are worthy" (Rev 3:4). I can imagine a tinge of jealousy and competitive fire igniting in the heart of the pastor. What would make them so special? Why are they approved by Jesus and called worthy?

Jesus mentions these members of the church not in order to shame or embarrass the pastor. He isn't pointing to them as if they are his favorite children and the pastor a second-rate failure. Jesus points them out as an encouragement and invitation. He describes the truest and best reputation one can have. Instead of believing the lies and putting on the mask that our activity earns our acceptance, these saints have believed the gospel, obeyed it, and abide in Christ. They've set down their attempts to earn a place of belonging and instead have received the gifts of Christ imparted by his Spirit through the Word.

Specifically, Jesus, first of all, identifies them as being in fellowship with him. They "walk with me." Their fellowship is a gift of love and belonging. Second, they walk in "white garments" signifying the gift of their justification and approval with God. They are in Christ, and being in Christ he gifts to them his perfect righteousness. Third, they are called worthy. The gift of dignity stands in their adoption in the family of God. An incredible and rich reputation and standing is theirs as gifts from God.

This is an encouragement and invitation to the pastor to possess the same gifts. So often we clamor for these realities ourselves: reputation, approval, and dignity. This is why we go off course so quickly. Our enemy isn't ignorant to what our hearts crave and long for. He just offers us cheap, fake substitutes for what realities could truly be ours.

While I was in college, I visited my parents living in Ecuador over Christmas break. One day as we were shopping in the city, I came across a small, hole-in-the-wall "store" that was selling all sorts of clothing and outdoor wear. Normally I'm not interested in shopping for clothing, but what caught my eye was the high-end, exclusive brand names they were selling. In the world of outdoor gear, the name North Face is one of the best-known, highest-quality, most expensive brands out there. A penniless college student like myself could hardly afford a North Face sticker. But there in the shop was a brand new, multi-layered, warm North Face winter coat that would usually retail for hundreds of dollars. All for the incredibly low price of thirty dollars. I bought it on the spot. Yet before I could even get through the first winter with my new North Face winter coat, it failed in its promise of keeping me warm and wore out rather quickly. My North Face coat was a disappointing North Fake.

Jesus doesn't offer us cheap, fake gifts. He offers the greatest and most glorious of realities. Just like the saints in Sardis who had not lived on a fabricated reputation that was all about activity and appearance, Jesus offers to the pastor a far better, eternal reputation: "The one who conquers will be clothed thus in white garments, and I will never blot his name out of the book of life. I will confess his name before my Father and before his angels" (Rom 3:5).

The pastor who abides in Christ will be rewarded with the reputation of righteousness. His name never being blotted of the book of life signifies an enteral citizenship and belonging. Having your name confessed before the Father is the pronouncement of dignity and worth before the King. A great name, approval, and dignity are all gifts that Jesus gives to the highest degree to those pastors who abide in him.

I want to be numbered among those who conquer. This means that I have to repent of my efforts to earn these gifts by my works.

Instead of curating a phony reputation or pretending that all is well and that I am sufficient enough for the weight of ministry, I have to turn instead to the one who enlivens and empowers ministry. I must repent of believing that my church's activity, size, status, budget, even reputation is the measure of my success. Instead, I need to "receive with meekness the implanted word, which is able to save" my soul (and my reputation!) (Jas 1:21).

Jesus says, "Let anyone who has ears to hear listen to what the Spirit says" (Rev 3:6 CSB). The Spirit is speaking the effective and life-giving word about our reputations and realities. Do we have ears to hear this about our condition and need? Could we turn and instead of being active for Christ learn to abide in Christ?

Abide with us, Lord, for it is toward evening, and the day is far spent.

Abide with us and with Your whole Church.

Abide with us at the end of the day, at the end of our life, and at the end of the world.

Abide with us with Your grace and goodness, with Your holy Word and Sacrament, with Your strength and blessing.

Abide with us when the night of affliction and temptation comes upon us, in the night of fear and despair, the night when death draws near.

Abide with us and with all the faithful, now and forever. Amen.[53]

AND TO THE angel of the church in Philadelphia write: "The words of the Holy One, the true one, who has the key of David, who opens and no one will shut, who shuts and no one opens.

"I know your works. Behold, I have set before you an open door, which no one is able to shut. I know that you have but little power, and yet you have kept my word and have not denied my name. Behold, I will make those of the synagogue of Satan who say that they are Jews and are not, but lie—behold, I will make them come and bow down before your feet, and they will learn that I have loved you. Because you have kept my word about patient endurance, I will keep you from the hour of trial that is coming on the whole world, to try those who dwell on the earth. I am coming soon. Hold fast what you have, so that no one may seize your crown.

"The one who conquers, I will make him a pillar in the temple of my God. Never shall he go out of it, and I will write on him the name of my God, and the name of the city of my God, the new Jerusalem, which comes down from my God out of heaven, and my own new name. He who has an ear, let him hear what the Spirit says to the churches."

REVELATION 3:7-13

CHAPTER SEVEN

PASTORS FIND THEIR VALUE IN JESUS

P astor, what's your value? How important are you?

I've heard it many times in various contexts, but the scenario works itself out something like this: In a room filled with hundreds, thousands, or even just a small few "elite" Christian leaders, someone will make a value statement of the success and worth of ministry based on its size, reach, or influence. This paragon of Christian leadership stands up and begins to tell the story of his church plant and its inauspicious beginnings. Sharing how he and his spouse were compelled to move into an area that had no engaging or strong Christian work, like the Messiah himself, they came to bring God's transformation to this down-and-out place.

The story shares a few notes of trial and a setback, details the sacrifices of the leader and his family, but then continues its triumphal victory parade to talk about how in time the church grew to a large, all-encompassing, world-changing "real" ministry. Inevitably the charisma of the speaker creates a reality distortion field around the listening audience, much like Steve Jobs could do with the release of whatever new iProduct he had invented. Soon everyone listening to the Christian leader is convinced of his entrepreneurial model of ministry, and specifically that the scope and size of his ministry are the definition and means of success. Like Pinocchio longing to be a "real boy," we hear these claims and wish to have a real church, if only we could push through the numerical ceiling above us. We long to finally reach the place where we are the ones who bring value to the church, where we have become an important voice in evangelicalism. We long to be the person who stands up and gives the rest of the world insight on how things are done in ministry. Instead of giving thanks for God's work in the ministry of another servant, we believe this is our birthright too, and we won't be anything of significance until we have it. We are discontent with the little flock God has given us to shepherd and instead long to "play big in the kingdom of God." When it seems to take decades (or even a few years from our initial start), we become frustrated with God. When we get to the great kingdom banquet, we're pretty sure he'll make us sit at the table for the little kids, while the big pastors get to talk about the important stuff with the rest of the saints.

The little pastor, hearing the voices of the American celebrity pastor, can feel his value is tied to the size of his church, the reach of his digital influence, or the prominence he has obtained in the world itself. Instead of hearing "Well done, good and faithful servant" (Matt 25:23), he is afraid he will hear, "You wicked and slothful servant" (Matt 25:26). The word "little," at least in our Western context, is often synonymous with "inadequate," even "bad." Working with little and being little in name and prominence cause us to wonder if we really even have the attention or smile of God. Will Jesus notice us when we all get to heaven?

HOLY, TRUE, PROMINENT

Jesus notices. And he shows up.

When Jesus reveals himself to the pastor of the church in Philadelphia in Revelation 3:7 he describes three realities about himself. Each of these realities becomes a multilayered statement about the significance of Jesus for the pastor. For the listening pastor, we receive a turning word away from our own prominence and value in the church and get a view of who should truly be the exalted one.

Jesus reveals himself as "the Holy One," a description of more than just his moral purity and integrity. He is the one set apart by God, for God; the one who is completely unique, absolutely distinct, one of a kind, and gloriously magnificent in every way. His majesty is unmatched and unrivaled.

Jesus is also "the true one." He proclaims himself as the genuine God and Lord. Beyond his integrity in always speaking the

truth, he reveals himself in contrast to a culture that offers counterfeit after counterfeit. He is the authentic and true God.

Jesus is the one "who has the key of David." With the key he
opens and shuts at his discretion, and there is not a soul in the
universe that can undo what he has done. The possessor of the
key of David is the one with the office, authority, and prominence
over the house of David. This is a title of lordship and authority.

When we see the Holy One, the true one, and the one who
has the key of David, what we see in reality is the divine Messiah.
We see the Christ, sent by God to save his people from their sins
and bring them into his eternal kingdom. The power of this vision
is to set before the pastor of Philadelphia a view of reality, so he
will see rightly when everyone else is telling him otherwise. Jesus
shows himself as truly the prominent one to beat back the lies of
a culture that says we make our own prominence.

LITTLE PHILADELPHIA

The ancient community of Philadelphia was no prominent place.
In fact, it was a city that struggled to keep its head above water.
Between catastrophic earthquakes and significant economic
upheaval, the city was the least prominent of the seven mentioned in Revelation 2–3.[54] The economy of the community was
built on the wool industry and the production of the vineyards
that benefited from the soil enriched by a nearby volcano.[55]

What gave Philadelphia importance was its location. The city
sat along a major commercial highway and "helped it earn the
title 'gateway to the East.'"[56] Because the city was a gateway for
the commercial and military movement of the Roman Empire,
it was also seen as a sending center, or "missionary city," for
the ideals, values, and culture of Rome to the eastern portions
of the Empire.[57]

Before the invention and the commercial use of the airplane,
cities like St. Louis, Missouri, functioned like ancient Philadelphia.
If you were a pioneer, trader, or someone looking for new land
or a fresh start away from the crowded East Coast, you would

inevitably travel through St. Louis. It was a bottleneck for commerce and trade into the Wild West. While not the largest city in our nation, it had a prominent place because it lay at the confluence of the Missouri and Mississippi rivers and in proximity to the confluence of the Ohio and Mississippi rivers. St. Louis was a launch point into new regions of the American continent.

We don't have much to go on about the church in Philadelphia, but from what we can tell it struggled with understanding its own prominence in the world, just like the city itself struggled. From what we can tell, the church wasn't a prominent church. It didn't seem to be a large and important ministry. Where other churches are mentioned elsewhere in the New Testament, even having epistles written directly to them (see Ephesians and Laodicea), Jesus' words to the church in Philadelphia found in Revelation 3:7–13 are the only scriptural reference to this church.

In Jesus' address to the pastor, he is full of affirmation. Of the seven letters, only this one and the one to the church in Smyrna having nothing but affirmation and encouragement for the pastors. There isn't a sin to repent of or a rebuke given. Jesus knows the church, and he knows his pastors and brings them exactly what they need. In this case Jesus again says, "I know your works" with approval and affirmation (3:8).

For some, especially those who despair of the smallness or seeming insignificance of their work, this kind of statement could be even more discouraging. "Yes, Jesus, I have sought to serve you as well as I could since I was ordained into ministry, but this is all I have for it. A few converts, some years spent praying and preaching and visiting, but we really didn't push past the two hundred barrier for Sunday morning attendance." Others may lament, "I tried to serve you well, but these people just don't seem to grow at all. We're always dealing with the same sin, the same brokenness, even the same problems. Nothing really seems to be changing."

Yet Jesus doesn't say, "I know your works," to bring shame or guilt. Instead, he takes the pastor of Philadelphia on a tour. Three times in this letter he tells the pastor to look or "behold." He wants the pastor of a smaller congregation in a less than impressive community to see things the way he sees them. There is no room for shame or guilt over the scope and size of your ministry. Jesus, the holy, true, and prominent one, wants you to see what he's doing.

BEHOLD THE OPEN DOOR

As Jesus tells pastors to look (behold), he shows us, first of all, a view of our unique place and prominence in perspective. "Behold, I have set before you an open door, which no one is able to shut" (Rev 3:8). While some may say this refers to the strategic calling and opportunity that Jesus has given to this church (similar to Paul's "open door" in Troas, 2 Cor 2:12), it is more likely that Jesus is alluding to a specific situation in the Old Testament in which the key of David is identified.

In Isaiah 22:15–23 God sends Isaiah to take a message to the steward of the king's household, Shebna. Isaiah is to tell Shebna that for his pride, self-reliance, and self-promotion he is going to be disposed of by God. Like being tossed by an Olympic hammer thrower, God tells Shebna he will whirl him "around and around, and throw [him] like a ball into a wide land" (Isa 22:18), casting him out. In his place God will call his servant Eliakim, and clothe him "with your robe, and will bind your sash on him, and will commit your authority to his hand. And he shall be a father to the inhabitants of Jerusalem and to the house of Judah. And I will place on his shoulder the key to the house of David. He shall open, and none shall shut; and he shall shut, and none shall open. And I will fasten him like a peg in a secure place, and he will become a throne of honor to his father's house" (vv. 21–23).

By making this reference in his word for the Philadelphian pastor, Jesus is reminding him of his sovereign authority both to depose and to set up. Specifically, Jesus wants the Philadelphian pastor to see that he has been given an office, a stewardship, and an authority that only Jesus himself can revoke. Even though the pastor has "little power," he was set in place by the Lord Jesus and his prominence is not to be measured in size, influence, or cultural power. His prominence is to be measured in terms of his office, given by God and affirmed by his faithfulness to his stewardship of Jesus' word and faithfulness to Jesus' name (Rev 3:8).

In the churches I have served as a pastor, an installation or commissioning service was usually held affirming my calling and laying out a charge in the duties I was assigned to take. After a few months of getting acquainted with the work and congregation of Woodside Bible Church in Plymouth, Michigan, a special time of dedication and prayer was set aside in our worship gatherings. A pastor from one of our other campuses came and gave me a word of calling and charge followed by several lay leaders from the congregation surrounding my wife and me, laying their hands on us, and commissioning us in prayer. Just one week earlier our senior pastor had given each of the campus pastors at Woodside a special coin. That coin was a representation of our calling to the leadership of a congregation of Woodside, a symbol of the character and integrity we are to uphold in our lives, and the fellowship we share as pastors with one another. The coin and the in-service dedication are confirmations by humans overseeing churches. Even more so, I have the confirmation that comes from the Lord, who calls me to himself, and directed us here through his providence. Because of these confirmations, I have a firm affirmation of my place in pastoral ministry and leadership at Woodside Bible Church.

When Jesus tells the Philadelphian pastor to behold the open door set before him, he is reminding him (and us) of Jesus' sovereign hand over our placement within the church. The message is important for us to see here: the size of your ministry, whether great or small, does not determine your value before the Lord or his sovereign authority in placing you where he has. You may have said yes to the call, but don't dismiss the ultimate hand of God in bringing you to the place where you serve. Behold your prominence in your placement by the King of kings.

BEHOLD THE LIES

The second thing Jesus calls the pastor to behold is the lies that are being said about where our value comes from. Jesus tells the pastor, "Behold, I will make those of the synagogue of Satan who say that they are Jews and are not, but lie" (Rev 3:9). This becomes an overlook for us to stop and see the folks that Jesus describes as liars. If the pastor was described as having "little power" just a moment earlier, these people are the ones with power. They are the prominent ones. They are the influencers. And they haven't really gone anywhere.

Influencers are all over the place today. The pastoral influencers can span the spectrum of theological orthodoxy, ministerial methodology, even onstage fashion. Every denominational network and theological community has its own version of these influencers. We all have our celebrity pastors that we seek approval and affirmation from. Chasing these influencers can bring a pressure down on us that distracts us from being faithful pastors. C. S. Lewis could have been talking about these influencers (and our desire to be among them) when he wrote the "Inner Ring."[58] These Inner Rings are, as Lewis described them, invisible circles of relationship that carry influence and community, which you may be included in or excluded from. Lewis comments, "I believe that in all men's lives at certain periods, and in many men's lives at all periods between infancy and extreme old age, one of the most dominant elements is the desire to be inside the local Ring and the terror of being left outside."[59]

No pastor I've ever met wants to be on the outside looking in on the real important stuff of the church in our cities and beyond. All of us have aspired at one time or another to be the next Charles Spurgeon, Billy Graham, or John Wesley—or pick your favorite pastor of prominence from history.

The pastor of the Philadelphian church had influencers bearing down on him as well. For his ministry the pressure of the influencers didn't come from within his own theological camp, nor was the pressure innate and passive. It was a direct assault of influence from an outside group seeking to intimidate and repudiate the church herself. The pastoral foe was a familiar one that even Jesus had to wage war against: the Jewish synagogue.

From Jesus' statement to Philadelphia's pastor it's clear the Jewish synagogue and its leadership were making life and ministry extremely difficult for this little church. If we read between the lines, it seems that they were seeking to rip up any stability of heart and mind that the Christians in the city might have longed for. Their assaults seem to have included telling the Christians that they were not loved by God, that instead God had chosen the Jews and established them as his people, and that there would be no place in the kingdom of heaven for these Christians. Many scholars believe the Jews of that city were telling the Roman authorities that the Christians were not Jews at all but a foreign and false faith that was in violent opposition to Rome because Christians proclaimed Jesus as Lord, not Caesar.[60] The influencers were pressuring the church to abandon its faith, forsake its union with Christ, and to run into the safe arms of Jewish practice and Roman allegiance.

I don't know if you see it, but these influencers of two thousand years ago are saying the same things to pastors today, some coming even from within our own tribes. The influencers tell pastors that God is love, and if we don't accept and affirm the alternative lifestyles of society today then we won't really be loved by God. The influencers shout that if your ministry isn't big then Jesus probably doesn't know your name, much less care about your labor for him. The influencers rant that cultural engagement, sensitivity, and accommodation are the surefire ways to win an audience, even if that means selling your soul to gain it. The influencers tell us that unless you're young, hip, have a hot band with a fog machine, and can relate to Gen-Z or millennials you should be put out to pasture and let the cool kids run the show now.

The influencers speak loudly, and they look great. They make it hard to be a faithful pastor these days. For younger developing leaders, the influencers seem to be the folks to follow. Who wants to listen to an older balding guy who has pastored for decades about how to be relevant in today's world? What in the world would a pastor who couldn't get more than one hundred people to show up for his sermons each week have to teach me about reaching the lost or planting a church or pastoring a congregation that Influencer Pastor couldn't say better? I mean, why even have that guy as a pastor? We have the technology now to all be able to listen to and watch the "Top Ten Influencer Pastors," who have never preached a bad message in their life. Let's get rid of the local church and local pastors and go all in on [insert favorite celebrity pastor's name here].

Jesus wants us to look and see the reality of what these influencers are. They are liars. Specifically, they lie about where your value and prominence come from. Jesus wanted the pastor of the church in Philadelphia to see the words about his prominence and belonging being placed in the wrong place as flat-out lies. What's staggering is that today's misinformation campaigns about our identity and prominence come from the same place: Satan. They are his lies and attacks, and Jesus, the one who is true, will expose these lies and deal decisively with this liar.

BEHOLD HIS LOVE

Jesus has a third thing for us to set our gaze on. He directs our attention to see what he, as the one who is holy, will do. What Jesus says to the pastor of Philadelphia is a dramatic reversal: "I know you have little power, and the Satanic Influencers are bearing down on you, but look! I will humble them before you and they will learn that I love you" (Rev 3:9).[61]

Jesus wants his pastors to see his love. Here we are recalled into our union with Christ. Our belonging to Jesus is drawn out and pressed home to our hearts. If we belong to Jesus, then we enjoy all the blessings that are associated with him. In this case, Jesus reminds us that belonging to him means we are loved by him.

Pastor, let that sink in. If you belong to Jesus, he loves you. No matter how big your church is, no matter how many followers and friends you have on social media, no matter if you play big or little in the kingdom of God, no matter how big of an impact you are having now or will in the future, Jesus loves you.

Jesus has for the Philadelphian pastor, and us today, a love that is infinite, beyond ourselves, bigger than our church size, broader than the scope of people we reach on our podcasts and livestreams, and deeper than the affirmation others can give us.

We need to see it! We need to behold how deeply Jesus loves us in the face of the lies that tell us our value is built on our church's size and prominence. Jesus doesn't love the pastor of the big church more than the one who has a smaller, less-well-known ministry. He doesn't delight more in the international traveler and evangelist who speaks to millions than he does the guy who speaks to the same fifty people every Sunday. His affections aren't attuned more to the brightest young stars in evangelicalism than they are to the unknown and forgotten pastors who labor faithfully in insignificant places.

Why can a pastor believe that and run to the bank with that kind of statement? Because he belongs to Jesus. What Jesus did in his own life of obscurity and relative insignificance is good news for both the pastor of little and the pastor of much. Jesus' sinless life and pursuit of his Father's glory laid the groundwork of his love by winning righteousness for all who believe. Jesus' suffering and sacrificial death on the cross paid for our own sins of arrogance and pride in attempts to build our own kingdom. Jesus' resurrection was validation of his sacrifice by the Father and brings the blessings he won to all who believe. By faith in God's grace, we are no longer strangers and enemies of God but his dearly beloved sons and daughters. John's statement at the beginning of his narrative of Jesus' final thirty-six hours illuminates the posture of Jesus toward us: "Having loved his own who were in the world, he loved them to the end" (John 13:1 CSB).

SECURE FOOTING IN THE LOVE OF GOD

Although Jesus has no critique or correction for the pastor of Philadelphia, he does have a call for him. Like a faithful coach coaxing his team along toward victory, Jesus gives a word to inspire and motivate this pastor on: "Hold fast what you have" (Rev 3:11). Jesus is telling us to keep going. Keep pressing on in what we have been called to do. Hold fast! Keep laboring in the places and among the people we have been given to minister to. Hold fast! Keep preaching the Word week in and week out. Hold fast! Keep pursuing holiness and Christlikeness in a world where compromise and capitulation are commonplace. Hold fast! Keep lifting up the holy and true King of kings. Pastor, keep faithfully serving your church.

Pastoring has always been something I've seen as a long-term calling. It's not a vocation that an individual should hop into just to climb a ladder of ministerial success, fame, and opportunity. Starting out in ministry, I had a perception of the pastorate and the church as similar to how coaching in collegiate football works. Coaches usually start out at the smaller schools in the lower divisions. If they are successful as a head coach, they may get an offer or be recruited to move up to a better conference and a larger school with a better program. If that goes well, another call comes along to an even larger school in a bigger conference with a better payday. Instead of staying at a school for a long time, the coach is evaluated annually and is either promoted or fired based on—you guessed it—results. Coaching at the collegiate level isn't building a long-term dynasty of equipping and building men for their lives. It's a short-term, win-or-go-home endeavor of climbing the ladder.

In many circles of American Christianity, the mentality of pastors and congregational leadership boards is the same. If the pastor grows the church and is successful, he'll get a calling from an even larger church in a more prominent place. If the church isn't growing like the board or congregation expected, the pressure mounts (sometimes internally in the pastor himself) for changes to be made, and for success to be found at any cost.

Many studies have pointed out that the average tenure of a pastor in one place is between five and seven years.

Now, I'm not saying there aren't very legitimate reasons for pastors to move on, or to be called to different and perhaps bigger churches. I'm not trying to say that leaders are unfaithful if they rightly discern the Lord's sovereign designs to relocate their ministry to another city and church. What I am saying is that often we need to be aware of our tendency to believe falsehoods that tell us our prominence comes from our upward mobility into larger and larger ministries. Jesus validates the prominence and platforms of the ministries we are currently in by his sovereign placement. Or, as I've heard it said many times, "shepherd the church you have now, not the one you hope to have."

Catch this, pastor: Christ has placed you in a strategic setting. The place you minister in right now might be in the middle of nowhere. City pastors may say if you're not in Los Angeles, New York, or Nashville you're just "downstream" from the culture they are pushing out from the cities. If you minister with a small church in "flyover country," you can be sure that the opportunities to preach and speak and "play big in the kingdom of God" are just going to sail over your head and land with the guy in the big places with the big churches. But where you are right now is the sovereign placement of Almighty God, who has positioned you in that community, with that church, for this time with an open door before you that no one else can shut.

It would be a betrayal of my calling if I didn't recognize that I was specifically called and placed (and the circumstances surrounding that call are absolute verification of that call in my life) at the church campus and community I am in right now in Plymouth, Michigan. I don't pastor the largest of the campuses, nor am I closest to the central leadership executives to be able to levy whatever strong influence I have. I pastor a smaller, perimeter church in the larger metro area. Yet I am confident of my calling, and have a significant awareness of the strategic uniqueness that makes up my campus's "open door" in the midst of Plymouth.

His calling on you right now isn't to chase the big church, or the big city (unless of course you live in the big city), or the big conference stage. His calling is for you to be faithful to the specific and strategic ministry that is right before your own two eyes. The apostle Peter reminds pastors to "shepherd the flock of God that is *among you*" (1 Pet 5:2). Because you belong to Jesus, you can labor in the little flock God has given. Francis Schaeffer said it well in his book *No Little People*, "As there are no little people in God's sight, so there are no little places. To be wholly committed to God in the place where God wants him—this is the creature glorified."[62] The place God has given you, the people he has called you to pastor—it is God's strategic and sovereign delight to place you among them. Hold fast to what you have.

SECURE IN OUR PROMINENCE

When we ask what our value is as pastors, and then determine that our value is somehow connected to the prominence and size of our ministries, we find ourselves on shifting ground. The ebb and flow of growth or decline will cause our hearts and egos to rise and fall as we evaluate each Sunday how many people did or did not show up at our churches.

Before the COVID-19 pandemic hit my region in 2020, my church had been experiencing a year-over-year pattern of at least 10 percent growth per year. The trends were all in the right direction. It felt good. I was confident in my pastoral leadership and was affirmed by how things were going. My inner voice was validating and even vindicating me against the lies that I had been told earlier in my career that I would never lead a church larger than one 125 members or be an effective leader. When the pandemic came along, navigating the difficulties of political, racial, and social disagreement caused our church attendance to significantly decline. At least a full third, if not closer to half, of our congregation left. My confidence was shattered. I began to question my own leadership. My heart sank. Nothing felt secure or prominent any longer.

Yet Jesus holds out a promise of stability and security for his pastors. For those in Christ our prominence is never tied to the highs or lows of attendance. Jesus promises pastors, as those who conquer, a secure and lasting place of prominence with him forever. Jesus says, "I will make him a pillar in the temple of my God. Never shall he go out of it" (Rev 3:12). In light of living in a city of diminished prominence and increased insecurity due to natural and economic problems, the promise to be established and secure in the very presence of God forever is attractive. Where else would be a more prominent place than in God's presence?

Beyond offering a secure presence in the most prominent place in the universe, Jesus holds out a prominent identity to us as well: "I will write on him the name of my God, and the name of the city of my God, the new Jerusalem ... and my own new name" (Rev 3:12). To be inscribed with God's name reveals belonging. To possess the name of God's city displays belonging to God's people. They are citizens of the kingdom of God. Having Jesus' own new name demonstrates intimacy and union.[63] This new threefold identity is given to utterly secure the pastor in his prominence. What higher realities could he possess? What greater prominence and place could be given to the faithful pastor who belongs to Jesus?

BECAUSE PASTORS BELONG TO JESUS, THEY CAN SERVE IN OBSCURITY

When anyone who has ears listens to what the Spirit says about our value and prominence, we can come to a deeper place of security and strength. Although the trends and voices of this world (and even the celebrity culture of the church) tell us that our value is relative to the size of our platforms, Jesus washes us with a better word. Although the desires build deeply within us for more listening ears, more online views, more invitations to be a big deal and a bigger and better influence, Jesus reminds us in our smallness that we are loved. Even though we may be tempted to hear the cry that big places are better, famous people are more prominent, and platform is all that matters, in Jesus we are secured in the highest of places, by the most prominent of Beings, upon an eternal platform of his love.

The pastor who remembers and receives the gospel word of Jesus, "I have loved you," can labor in the little places of obscurity (even if they are in the middle of the big city) among people of insignificance and weakness because our value comes from Christ, not from our budget, buildings, or how many butts fill the seats of our auditoriums. Our value comes from Christ.

Pastor, labor where you are planted. The door of opportunity that only Christ can give is open before you. He has ordained before the foundation of the earth good works for you to do in the church you are in right now. Rest in the love of Jesus, and labor to feed his little flock that he died to purchase for himself.

AND TO THE angel of the church in Laodicea write: "The words of the Amen, the faithful and true witness, the beginning of God's creation.

"I know your works: you are neither cold nor hot. Would that you were either cold or hot! So, because you are lukewarm, and neither hot nor cold, I will spit you out of my mouth. For you say, I am rich, I have prospered, and I need nothing, not realizing that you are wretched, pitiable, poor, blind, and naked. I counsel you to buy from me gold refined by fire, so that you may be rich, and white garments so that you may clothe yourself and the shame of your nakedness may not be seen, and salve to anoint your eyes, so that you may see. Those whom I love, I reprove and discipline, so be zealous and repent. Behold, I stand at the door and knock. If anyone hears my voice and opens the door, I will come in to him and eat with him, and he with me.

"The one who conquers, I will grant him to sit with me on my throne, as I also conquered and sat down with my Father on his throne.

"He who has an ear, let him hear what the Spirit says to the churches."

REVELATION 3:14-22

CHAPTER EIGHT

PASTORS
REPENT

"What are you teaching the congregation?"

The question wasn't about my sermon texts. I wasn't being asked to do an evaluation of my doctrine to see if I was majoring on the minors or getting on a theological hobby horse and riding it off into the sunset every Sunday. The question came from a speaker during a workshop on our worship services asking us to think about what the practice of our services was teaching. Beyond the subject matter of my sermons, I was being reminded that everything we do in worship communicates and ultimately teaches something. Our songs teach how we view praise and adoration. Our prayers teach how we should approach God and our view of our need. The way I handle Scripture instructs the church about how to read and approach the Bible for themselves. Yes, we are actually praying and adoring and giving, but what we do in a service is also training our people how to live through the week. The workshop speaker was correct in pointing out that everything—absolutely everything—communicates something.

Including my omissions.

The elements of gathered worship that I leave out, gloss over, or dismiss tell our people something. It is one thing to have a high view of Scripture and preach expositionally through larger sections of Scriptures and give time and verbal affirmation to that value. It is another thing to say nothing about our need, being dependent on the Lord, or actually praying for the "daily bread" that Jesus instructs us to pray for. My omission would eventually catch up with me.

In the first several years of my pastoral tenure in Michigan, I found I was pastoring in an affluent community. As a church that was in a season of revitalization and renewal, it was exciting to me that more and more people were coming each weekend. The room was filling up and people were giving. Each week when I received the giving report from our campus, I was thrilled to discover that once again the congregation's generosity had surpassed the weekly budgeted need for our church. This wasn't just a week or two followed by a hopeful and urgent cry in the last few months of the fiscal year to make up any deficits we were running. The excessive generosity went on for several years. I was proud that I didn't have to talk about giving and money to my congregation. Instead of mentioning the offering each Sunday, I began to assume it. We were in a rich community that was generous and knew how to give. Why did I need to say or do anything about it?

I didn't realize that by my omission I was teaching our church something: self-reliance.

It wasn't until year three that the church was no longer keeping up with the weekly need. Our congregation had grown. Our budget was modest but had grown as well. Yet we weren't making ends meet. That's when the gracious timing of the Lord brought me into the question the workshop speaker was raising. What was I teaching my congregation?

As I analyzed the question and evaluated the elements of our worship service, I realized we were missing something important. I was expecting the offerings to be stable and significant, but I was focused on the self-reliance and affluence of the congregation to provide those funds. I wasn't teaching our congregation *anything* about the source of all that we have. I wasn't inviting them to go the Lord and express humility and faith for him to provide our daily and week-to-week sustenance, whether that was food to eat or a budget to meet. By my omission I was teaching the church that we didn't need God to provide for us as we gave, we just needed our givers to reach into their pockets and write a check.

I needed to repent, and I had to do it publicly. The omission of prayer in our services, even for something as small and brief as our offering, was an act of pride and a leadership failure on my part. I had to reorient our church to being dependent on the Lord for everything, and I owned my responsibility in leading them into an attitude of self-reliance.

So I led us in prayer. I shared with the congregation my self-reliant attitude and asked them to forgive me for failing to reinforce that "it is the Lord who will provide." I prayed week after week with faith-filled prayers asking God to supply what we need for ministry, for the poor, and for the advance of the gospel around the world.

The act of confessing my sin and asking for forgiveness wasn't anxiety-inducing in this setting, but it could have been. Confession of sin and repentance puts us in a new light with others. We have to be open, vulnerable, even weak to say we struggle and wrestle with sin. Having our congregations see us for the normal and sinful humans we are instead of the superior and nearly infallible leaders we desire ourselves to be is tense. Doing heart work on our own souls, especially when it comes to sin, is dangerous. We don't like it. Repentance feels like unsafe territory. At least that's what we've been deceived into thinking.

Much of our upside-down thinking about our belonging in pastoral ministry comes from the way we've mistakenly formulated the gospel for ourselves. We've believed the double lie that if we perform well, we will belong. If we are enough, we will belong to Jesus. And it's those lies that have robbed, yes *robbed*, us of the liberating and safe means of grace that God has given us in repentance. In fact, I may be so bold to say the pastors who are the most secure in their belonging to Christ are the ones that undertake the means of grace in repentance with regularity. Yet it's the fear of revealing our sin that often keeps us from being repentant leaders.

THE UN-SELF-AWARE SOUL

When Jesus gets into it with his pastors and the churches, he's not ignorant of the issues he's going to be dealing with. He's not surprised that he has to uncover, correct, and mend sin. What surprises us is how the people he corrects seem blind and ignorant to their own sin. How could they not know it as well?

In the last of the letters to the seven pastors, in Revelation 3:14–22, Jesus turns his attention to the pastor of the Laodicean church. It's a stern letter, frankly, almost as if Jesus has filed a lawsuit and taken this pastor to court. Jesus puts himself on the witness stand to speak to this pastor. In this instance, Jesus describes himself very directly. He is "the Amen, the faithful and true witness" (Rev 3:14). He is direct in making sure the pastor has a grasp on who is actually telling the truth. The very things Jesus says are God's truth. He rightly measures up, understands, assesses, and judges the situation. He is the true witness. No lies will be spoken from his mouth about the condition of the Laodicean pastor.

When Jesus describes himself as "the beginning of God's creation" (Rev 3:14) he is affirming his right and rulership over all things. The identification of himself, which would have been familiar to the Laodiceans as one of the congregations to receive Paul's Letter to the Colossians (Col 4:16), was an identification of his supreme rank over all things. "In their wealth and complacency, they thought of themselves as in control; Jesus is telling them that he alone controls creation; he is the very source of their wealth and power."[64]

Both truth and position were needed to expose the deception and lack of soul-awareness that existed in the heart of the Laodicean pastor's life. The words "the Amen, the faithful and true witness, the beginning of God's creation" are necessary to reveal what otherwise has been hidden or ignored. Jesus is precisely who he needs to be for this church and their pastor in that moment.

The staggering problem with the Laodicean ministry was just how blind the church was to its own condition. The pastor had one view of the church; the Lord had a very different perspective. The city itself was one of the wealthiest cities in the entire region. It was situated on the crossroads of two major highways that brought all of the commercial benefit of the Roman Empire through their gates. Economically, the city was a prosperous banking and exchange center. Culturally, it had a distinctive fashion industry because of the unique black wool that was produced there. In regard to health care, Laodicea was a leading-edge city in the production of medicinal ointment for eyes.

In AD 60 a major earthquake hit the city, leveling everything. Because the city was so affluent and self-reliant, instead of receiving government aid from Rome, the city declined. They had all the resources they needed to rebuild the city.[65] In their eyes they did not need anything from anywhere or anyone else.

This cultural self-reliance didn't just exist as part of the secular fabric of the city of Laodicea. It was as much part of the cultural fabric of the pastor and the church itself. Just like the city, the church was self-sufficient and self-reliant. The pastor himself embodied this identity. In many conservative and capitalistic contexts, this self-reliant and self-sufficient posture might seem like a great thing. One marker of success in church-planting today is when a church can become fiscally self-sufficient and self-supporting. While the fiscal independence of a church is one thing, spiritual self-reliance is nothing to be praised. In fact, it's sickening.

Much is made about the metaphor Jesus picks up to indict the pastor in Laodicea. The debate over what the temperature of the water signifies is tertiary to the real issue. Their spiritual condition is such that Jesus tells the pastor he will spit them out of his mouth. The real problem is his un-self-aware soul. Jesus quotes the pastor and church directly: "You say, I am rich, I have prospered, and I need nothing" (Rev 3:17).

Unfortunately, it was all a delusion.

To Jesus, the church and this pastor are vomit-inducing. The pastor can say he is rich, prospering, and self-sufficient but Jesus knows he is just the opposite: "wretched, pitiable, poor, blind, and naked" (Rev 3:17). Lacking clear soul-awareness, the pastor has developed a faulty dashboard of health and let its results drive him into the darkness.

WHY CAN'T WE SEE?

It's worth asking, why the gap here? What was it in the pastor's life that caused him to be so unaware of the condition of his own soul? Sure, he may have had money in the bank, but he didn't have treasure in heaven. His life translated over into a culture within the church as well. What the congregation sees the leaders of the church teach and practice, they too teach and practice. The result of a leader that was blind to his own soul was a church that was blind to its own condition. Yet how could the pastor of the church be so blind?

The conclusion is that sin's power deceives. The writer of Hebrews reminds us that sin is deceitful in its very constitution (Heb 3:13). We can't spiritually see when we are allured into the deceits of sin. Our desires are engaged in the seductive promises that sin makes, and when our desires are engaged we can't see clearly.

Still, I'm confident that the Laodicean pastor didn't walk in on day one and say to his leadership team, "Church, I'm about to drive us into spiritual darkness with my aggressive five-year plan." It was more likely a movement of degrees. Bit by bit, unchecked, undiscerned, unperceived, the church moved from the moorings of faithfulness to the unsteady waters of worldly whims. Spiritual erosion crept in through seemingly insignificant decisions: expediency over character, pragmatics over convictions, production over principles, comparison over contentment. Like cataracts slowly clouding the eye of the soul, each degree of departure led further into spiritual blindness.

This should sober us as pastors. It's not that we come into our ministry roles determined to take the church into immorality and darkness. I highly doubt that you want the legacy of your ministry to be spiritual disaster. No one aims for that. Yet we drift. We take spiritual shortcuts. We choose the convenient over the cross. We measure ourselves by the success standards of the church-growth movement instead of the ordinary faithfulness of the cruciform way. We long for the day when we can be spiritually self-reliant, and our souls can stretch out into their own self-sufficiency. If Jesus will show up and give us his vote of approval, all will be well. Instead, we're making the choices of blindness.

I have to wonder if Jesus were to show up at our churches, would he vomit?

REVELATION THAT REVERSES

When Jesus told the Laodicean pastor he was delusional about his condition, and the condition of the church, it had to be a gut punch for him. There is no success in hearing, "I will spit you out of my mouth" (Rev 3:16). Yet the light of the faithful and true witness was shining on the blinded soul of this shepherd to bring healing and restoration. Revelation brings revelation. We all need the light shining on our hearts.

This is a necessary step for us in doing the work of repentance. Obtaining an accurate self-awareness of our soul, and regularly checking our blind spots, is a means of standing in the light of the truth. Just as Jesus did this for the pastor of Laodicea, so each of us needs others who will pastor our souls well by bringing us into the light with the revelation of the truth. And this is the step that is most frightening to us.

Perhaps you think of this light-shining, truth-telling operation a bit like the conventional accountability practices that I was exposed to growing up. As I went through adolescence the Promise Keepers movement was in full swing inviting men to fill stadiums, get right with God, and then keep each other accountable, mainly to avoid pornography, each week. The movement made its impact on the church as groups of men with "accountability partners" would meet and ask the Questions.

The Questions, derived from a prominent pastor, focused mainly on behavioral practices that assume the worst possible interpretation. "Have you been with a woman anywhere this past week that might be seen as compromising? Have you exposed yourself to any sexually explicit material? Have any of your financial dealings lacked integrity?" Finally, the survey concluded with an ominous you-can't-get-out-of-jail-free inquiry: "Have you just lied to me?" While there was some success with these accountability groups, it was behavioral modification at the best, based on the tactics of law and fear. Repentance became painful and fearful, lest you be found faithless and a liar.[66]

But that's not how Jesus draws us into the light. He doesn't sit us down in a dark room with a bright lamp shining over us while he interrogates us to see if we will confess to what he already knows. He doesn't treat us as a captured terrorist against the kingdom of God with threats to be waterboarded unless we give up the goods on our wayward heart. His way of drawing us into the light is to invite us into far greater joys than the ones we currently possess. Jesus draws it out of us with compassion, gentleness, and a replacing sweetness that overcomes the bitter obstinance of our hearts.

Jesus speaks to the pastor perceiving his own prosperity, self-sufficiency, and worldly well-being saying, "Friend, you are very sick. You're actually pathetic and poor and blind and naked. But let me counsel you to buy (at no cost even!) better goods from me. I've got the best." What makes it safe for the pastor to repent is that the one bearing witness against him is also applying the remedy to him. While Jesus knows the heart's condition, he also knows and offers the life-restoring antidote to the soul sickness of prosperity. He doesn't bark, command, insult, or incite fear. He invites us into a better condition by shining the light on our desperate need and directing us to where that need is met.

In verse 18, Jesus highlights the cultural realities of the city of Laodicea. As a banking center, the city was filled with the currency of Rome. So Jesus invites the pastor to buy gold from him, instead of having "faith in the bank and money in his heart."[67] As the city flourished as a fashion center that would rival modern Milan, Jesus invites the pastor to reject the garments of the world and buy garments of righteousness to clothe his spiritual nakedness. Instead of parroting the self-sufficiency of the medical community producing ointment to cure poor eyesight, Jesus lays out wisdom, calling the pastor to a cure for spiritual blindness through the salve that only he offers. In each case Jesus calls for a rejection of the world's offer of sufficiency through prosperity and instead invites us into better life found in his sufficiency.

Pastor, this is the kind of revelation that brings out repentance. The apostle Paul was correct in his assertion that "God's kindness is meant to lead you to repentance" (Rom 2:4). It's the sort of kindness Christ wants to bring to our lives. Jesus wants us to see just how enough he is, so that we'll stop trifling around with the trinkets of this world. Richard Sibbes reminds us that repentance is "not a little hanging down our heads ... but a working our hearts to such a grief as will make sin more odious unto us than punishment."[68]

But it comes with a cost. The counsel that Christ gives us is to "buy from me" the only things that will heal our sin-sick hearts (Rev 3:18). How do we do that? What's the currency that we must use to buy from Christ his healing remedies?

Only that we come to Christ himself.

Jesus' words remind us of the invitation God gave through the prophet Isaiah: "Come, everyone who thirsts, come to the waters; and he who has no money, come, buy and eat! ... Seek the LORD while he may be found; call upon him while he is near; let the wicked forsake his way, and the unrighteous man his thoughts; let him return to the LORD, that he may have compassion on him, and to our God, for he will abundantly pardon" (Isa 55:1, 6–7).

Here's the template for our repentance: come empty-handed to Jesus, seek him, call on him, forsake your old way, and return to him. The results are magnificent: compassion, abundant pardon, complete forgiveness! But we must come, and we must buy from him. We must repent.

REPROVED BECAUSE YOU BELONG

You might balk at the idea that repentance is safe, especially for the pastor. We've heard (and probably lived) the stories of pastors confessing with a close friend their sins and the "friend" betraying that trust by spreading the news "for the good of the church." The perception is that it is even less safe if the church board gets involved. Overall character is questioned, punitive measures are discussed, trust is eroded, and if anything, the pastor may be out of a job before he has a chance to reach the pulpit the following Sunday. The economic, societal, and spiritual fallout that occurs in the life of a pastor and his family is more than enough motivation to keep the pastor's sins suppressed deep down. We believe it's not safe for a pastor to confess his sin.

This concern, though, is an indictment on the church, not on the practice of repentance itself. When repentance is met with betrayal, punishment, and expulsion, we get it all wrong. Consider what Jesus says to the pastor that he was discipling in Laodicea. "Those whom *I love*, I reprove and discipline" (Rev 3:19).

Jesus concludes his testimony against the pastor by affirming his love for him. He wouldn't be speaking to Laodicea about its self-sufficiency and opulent idolatry if he didn't love them. He brings his discipline to the heart of this pastor *because* he loves him. The love of Christ for his own regulates the way in which he deals with the sin that destroys his beloved people. Discipline from Christ is bound up in his love for his people. It's a different kind of correction altogether.

We usually think of discipline as a corrective measure to make sure people do the right thing. Discipline is a means of correcting what is wrong so that the wrongdoer will be transformed into a right-doer. Under this model of correction, those who have failed are put under the corrective eye of those who are superior in their behavioral performance. The "correction" is a matter of levying some punitive measures that will inflict a level of pain, loss, and retribution on the offender.

Poor Ralphie Parker's experience with discipline in the iconic holiday film *A Christmas Story* paints a familiar scene. After hearing again and again his father's expletive-laced tirades, which are "still hanging in space over Lake Michigan," against their house's malfunctioning furnace, Ralphie picks up a few new vocabulary words to try himself. When his moment of manhood comes by helping his father change a flat tire on the side of the road, he ends up mishandling the lug nuts only to let out "the queen mother of dirty words," which of course he had learned from his father. The disappointment and terror are palpable. Corrective discipline comes in the form of sucking on a bar of soap in an effort to clean out his mouth. This type of discipline aims at external behaviors, as if soap could wash out the tongue of all filthy talk.

When we think of God disciplining us, we assume that he's out just to change us into people who do the right things. Yes, the wrong-doers will be punished, and the right-doers will be rewarded. But do wrong enough, and eventually you'll be kicked out of the house.

Jesus isn't merely about correcting the behavior that makes us bad. He knows that the sin that corrupts us is not merely what we do but is entrenched in our very hearts. Dealing with us harshly, or externally, won't make us better people. He has to get us on the operating table and do radically invasive surgery. The question is, Will we be open to his surgical methods? Will we submit ourselves to his procedure for dealing with corrupt hearts?

This is why repentance, for the pastor, can be so difficult. We know we're going to be scrutinized more carefully. We know the cuts may need to go deeper. We know our indwelling sin may be subtler and more socially acceptable than the sins of the people within our congregations. But that is what makes those sins all the more dangerous.

What problem did Jesus find with the Laodicean pastor that would call him to say in essence, "You make me feel sick?" Gross sexual immorality? Heresy? False teaching? Spiritual apathy? None of these! Jesus sees a pastor whose sins have become so subtle that discerning them apart from the community he is in may almost be impossible. The subtle sins of self-sufficiency and desire for affluence and success sit deeper in the heart than the behaviors of adultery and murder. It's going to take more than a bar of soap in the mouth to cure the soul cancer that dwells within.

Only love can draw out this kind.

Jesus stands on the relationship he has with this pastor to draw him into repentance. The affirmation of love is not missing or withheld: "Those whom I love, I reprove and discipline."

Maybe feeling the tinge of your conscience as you consider your heart is difficult. Perhaps the nudging of the Holy Spirit in conviction of your sins makes you feel uncomfortable. Being challenged to confess the pride within your soul brings out defensiveness and reluctance. If you would be self-aware enough to recognize those sins, then you can be assured of safety in repenting of those sins to Jesus. Those acts of discipline are demonstrations of his love. And in them is complete security.

That is the motivation for repentance. I am so completely and totally loved by Jesus that nothing in this world can unseat or diminish his love for me. If anything, I am so secure in Jesus that I can show him all my failures, and he will tenderly and gently go to work healing me. He won't turn me away.

Jesus loves me. So I can tell him anything. Jesus loves me. I can own up to my greatest failures. Jesus loves me. I can renounce myself. Jesus loves me. I can stop seeking approval of others. Jesus loves me. I can reject this world and all that it has to offer. Jesus loves me. He disciplines me. And since there is nothing that can stop him from loving me, and nothing that can take me out of his hands, I can "be zealous and repent!" (Rev 3:19).

WHAT HAPPENS WHEN WE REPENT?

How does Jesus get us to repentance? He patiently stands at the door and knocks. His method of bringing us to repentance is shared by his motivations for our repentance. Because he loves us, he acts in love to draw us to repentance.

When it comes to repentance, we often think of the story of the prodigal son (Luke 15:11–32). The youngest son tells his dad he wishes he was dead, takes his share of his inheritance, runs off and squanders all of it only to return to his senses when he is utterly destitute in poverty and shame. Upon his return, the father welcomes him with open arms, throws a big party, and restores the son. It's a fitting picture of the Lord's reception of a wayward sinner.

But that's not the picture Jesus uses to invite the Laodicean pastor into repentance. The pastor wouldn't see himself as a lost, wayward, destitute son. No, the banquet room at the Laodicean church was packed out. The affluence ran thick. The party had already been going on for quite some time. Yet the guest of honor was missing. In fact, the guest of honor had been uninvited. But that didn't mean Jesus was going to _not_ show up.

He _does_ show up, but he doesn't barge in. He's there but refrains from forcing himself on the host. He stands outside the door, and he knocks. Jesus' picture of himself knocking at the door is profound because it suggests that he desires to have fellowship with us. In the same letter in which he told the pastor of this local church, "I will spit you out of my mouth," he also states he wants to be in fellowship with that pastor. This is no contradiction. Jesus' aim of love is our repentance so that our relationship can be restored. Because he loves us, he knocks.

But what happens next? How do things play out when the two estranged parties look into each other's eyes? I've had the sad experience of trying to figure out what to do when I've unexpectedly crossed paths with someone who has wronged me. If our eyes meet, we look away from each other. There's a recognition that we're in the same room, but not a desire to be in the same room. If we are at a social gathering, we visually keep tabs on each other as we circle the place, hoping to not come into contact, or worse, to have to talk with the other. There's a knowing agreement to keep the fake peace, but not a desire to mend the fence.

Is that what it's like with Jesus when we open the door and acknowledge our sins? Does he keep his eyes on us to make sure we don't get too close, while being barely empathetic enough to share the space with us?

Not according to Jesus. He knocks, we hear, we open, he enters, and "I will come in to him and eat with him, and he with me" (Rev 3:20). When we open the door in repentance, Jesus comes right into the dining room where the meal is being served and pulls up a chair, and we sit down together and eat and drink as old, faithful friends. Forgiveness is clear and applied. It's as if there was never any separation between us. The relationship has been restored, the sin forgiven, even forgotten, and deep friendship and fellowship carry on.

The spiritual reality of forgiveness carries itself out in faith-filled knowledge that "if we confess our sins, he is faithful and just to forgive us our sins and to cleanse us from all unrighteousness" (1 John 1:9). But when we confess our sins to others in true repentance we can hear verbally and experience the reality of forgiveness that comes with repentance. Just as we speak a word of absolution and forgiveness to those who sin against us and repent, so we need to have spoken to us the words of absolution and forgiveness by friends in our own repentance.

I have found the practice of daily Morning Prayer with the Book of Common Prayer to be a helpful and needed retuning of my heart to my sin, my need, and the forgiveness that only Jesus supplies. In the General Confession each morning, I lay out again the reality that "we have followed too much the devices and desires of our own hearts. We have offended against thy holy laws. We have left undone those things which we ought to have done; And we have done those things which we ought not to have done; And there is no health in us." But I also get to hear and receive the words, "The Almighty and merciful Lord grant you absolution and remission of all your sins, true repentance, amendment of life, and the grace and consolation of his Holy Spirit."

This dynamic is even more deeply realized when we have others in our lives with whom we can share our confession and from whom we can hear this absolution. Find a pastor who can pastor you. You need to hear the word of grace about your soul from the lips of an embodied person telling you of your forgiveness and belonging in Christ.[69] Enjoying renewed fellowship with Christ is mediated through his Word as we partake of him and through his people as they proclaim to us the hope and remedy of the gospel to our repentant hearts.

FINDING VICTORY

Jesus' command to repent comes with a promise. When we sin there is the terrible tremor of lies that tells us we'll never make it. We're afraid we'll never have a victory, never truly be overcomers, never be first-class citizens of heaven. Yet Jesus' final promise is perhaps his most precious one. It wipes out completely any of the lies or deceptions we may carry about our standing with him. To the one who conquers Jesus promises, "I will grant him to sit with me on my throne, as I also conquered and sat down with my Father on his throne" (Rev 3:21).

The brilliance of this promise is revealed in Jesus' call to the Laodicean pastor, and to us. To overcome is to be a pastor of repentance. As Jesus calls us to "be zealous and repent," so he promises that those who do will receive the reward of victory.

To sit on Jesus' throne (which is the same throne as the Father) is to receive and stand in his victorious triumph. It is the promise of being glorified with Christ on the last day and enjoying in our union with Christ all the benefits and glories that are his. The promise reminds us that "he who began a good work in you will bring it to completion at the day of Jesus Christ" (Phil 1:6). Just as Jesus conquered, so he reminds us we will conquer in him and enjoy the entirety of victory that he enjoys.

The key to overcoming and taking hold of this promise is repentance. It is the mark of a humble pastor who knows who he is and knows the power and reality of Christ's redemptive grace. Jesus invites us into his victory by acknowledging our need constantly, and by faith taking hold of what his word promises.

"Let anyone who has ears to hear listen to what the Spirit says" (Rev 3:22 CSB).

This is what Jesus wants for you, pastor. He wants to enjoy the table fellowship and communion of heart with you, even now. He stands and knocks. He calls to you, "Repent, believe the good news!" as he waits for you to come to the door and open it. And you can! Hear this voice and open the door. Because you belong to Jesus, you can repent. Because you are safe in his affections, safe in his affirmation, safe in his approval, you can repent of all your sin. The safest thing to do in all the world may feel like the least safe thing to do, but because you belong to Jesus and because he is enough, you can repent.

AFTER THIS I looked, and behold, a door standing open in heaven! And the first voice, which I had heard speaking to me like a trumpet, said, "Come up here, and I will show you what must take place after this." At once I was in the Spirit, and behold, a throne stood in heaven, with one seated on the throne. And he who sat there had the appearance of jasper and carnelian, and around the throne was a rainbow that had the appearance of an emerald. Around the throne were twenty-four thrones, and seated on the thrones were twenty-four elders, clothed in white garments, with golden crowns on their heads. From the throne came flashes of lightning, and rumblings and peals of thunder, and before the throne were burning seven torches of fire, which are the seven spirits of God, and before the throne there was as it were a sea of glass, like crystal.

And around the throne, on each side of the throne, are four living creatures, full of eyes in front and behind: the first living creature like a lion, the second living creature like an ox, the third living creature with the face of a man, and the fourth living creature like an eagle in flight. And the four living creatures, each of them with six wings, are full of eyes all around and within, and day and night they never cease to say,

"Holy, holy, holy, is the Lord God Almighty,
    who was and is and is to come!"

And whenever the living creatures give glory and honor and thanks to him who is seated on the throne, who lives forever and ever, the twenty-four elders fall down before him who is seated on the throne and worship him who lives forever and ever. They cast their crowns before the throne, saying,

"Worthy are you, our Lord and God,
    to receive glory and honor and power,
for you created all things,
    and by your will they existed and were created."

REVELATION 4:1–11

CHAPTER NINE

PASTOR, JESUS IS ENOUGH

There we were, room half empty, congregation splintered and fractured. My heart was discouraged because friends had left. What I had spent my energy over the prior five years building evaporated seemingly overnight. I wasn't enough.

I've been learning I don't have to be.

When I set out to write these chapters on Jesus' letters to his pastors, I knew I might face some experiences that would test and prove these truths in my own life. I had no clue that I was going to face the most difficult two-year stretch of ministry I've ever had. It's as if the Spirit was asking me if *I* had ears to hear. Did I really believe the enoughness of Jesus for my own life and ministry?

I've never thought of myself as having a small view of Jesus. Yet, in the space of those twenty-four months, I've realized I may have had a functional view of Jesus' greatness. He was good enough to turn water into wine and to heal the lame, blind, bleeding, dying, and dead. Jesus was exalted in his great wisdom and pure and perfect words. Jesus' compassion toward sinner and sufferer revealed his solidarity with humanity. Jesus in his suffering and sacrifice displayed cosmic, universe-altering love for the world, and rescues us from the fate of eternal wrath and hell. His resurrection displays his power and victory over Satan, sin, and death.

All these things were there in the pages of Scripture as holy and true, the very Word of God. I could say Jesus was enough. But my experience of Jesus being enough *for me* as a pastor was limited in its range. Perhaps that's true for you as well. I know I'm not the only one who has been through deep waters and great tribulation as a pastor. My conversations with pastors in the last few years have ranged from those in the first year of their church plants that struggled with Jesus' enoughness to seasoned veterans with decades of ministry experience behind them. One pastor who has been in ministry for over forty years told me that 2020 and 2021 were the toughest two years of ministry he had ever experienced. We're all asking what happened. We're all eager to recover.

If anything, we've all faced the trial of believing Jesus is enough. Maybe we've experienced his enoughness through the pressures and difficulties of pastoral ministry and have grown in our capacity to entrust ourselves to him even more. Perhaps we're still on the way and need the Spirit to work these realities deeper into our hearts. Maybe as you have read these reflections on our belonging to Jesus and how that works itself out in our lives, you've become discouraged. The calls in ministry to love Jesus most, suffer, become like Jesus, teach and tell the truth, abide in Christ, labor in little, and repent may feel like more added pressure to perform and be enough for your church. You just want some hope.

WHAT TO SAY AFTER THOSE LETTERS?

I can imagine the seven pastors who received these letters convening at a conference together. Their mail has been read by everyone in the church. In fact it's *the word* on the churches, spoken out by the Lord of the church himself. There's no fallacy in his evaluation of his pastors and their churches.

The pastors may be a little embarrassed, maybe a bit ashamed. Two of them are encouraged, but they still bear the pain of suffering and the marks of affliction on their lives. Two of them have been reproved for being either dead or lukewarm: the work ahead of them is significant and deep. Nevertheless, Jesus has spoken to each of them as his, and called them to receive and embrace his sufficiency for them and their churches. He's given each of them realities of himself and promises to motivate their faith and obedience.

I can image them sitting around a table asking, "What's next? Are we going to make it? Is there hope for us?" If Revelation was merely these first three chapters, we would have seven letters and seven invitations, but we'd be left incomplete. Many commentaries formulate an outline of Revelation with divisions occurring between chapter 3 and 4. There is a unity to the book, but even in my own preaching of these texts I've concluded the series at the end of chapter 3. "Repent. Open the door to Jesus. Get on with the work of being enough for your church."

But we should keep going in the text. The conclusion occurs when "Amen" is said. Jesus isn't done showing how much he is enough for us.

Revelation opens with John at Patmos receiving a command to write to the seven pastors. With this command, the resurrected, ascended Jesus shows himself in his glory to John. Held in his hand are the pastors of the churches. The message is clear: pastors, you belong to Jesus.

Now, at the conclusion of his sovereign word to each pastor and his church, a new vision unfolds. John is taken up to heaven, right into the throne room with "one seated on the throne" (Rev 4:2). There is no doubt who this one is on the throne. John is in the presence of Almighty God. Radiant majesty is his appearance (v. 3) and triumphant power is his dominion (v. 5). The Spirit of God is active in his presence before the throne interceding on behalf of his people (Rom 8:26–27). The highest order of angelic hosts stands nearest to the throne at each corner. "The LORD reigns! ... Let the heavens be glad, and let the earth rejoice" (Ps 96:10–11).

John sees more than this. There surrounding the singular throne are twenty-four thrones. Seated on these thrones are "twenty-four elders" (Rev 4:4). If we could suspend any attempts at trying to give a precise explanation of exactly who these elders are for the moment, I'd like for us to consider the term used to identify them: "elders." The same title used throughout the New Testament to signify the pastors of the churches is used here.[70]

I am glad that John identifies the ones around the throne as elders. Yes, it's probably a symbolic representation of the entire people of God, but isn't that what being an elder or pastor is? Are we not a representative of God to his people? Don't we function as overseers of the people of God, shepherding the people of God as ones who keep watch over their souls (1 Pet 5:1–2; Heb 13:17)?

The identity is specific and not just symbolic. There, surrounding the throne of God, are the pastors of Jesus' church. They are wearing the garments of righteousness that he promised those who overcome (Rev 3:5), the crowns of royalty and life he promised to the faithful, suffering pastor on their head (Rev 2:10).

Just as Jesus in the first vision stood here on earth in the midst of the seven churches with the seven pastors, so now in heaven the throne of God is surrounded by the elders and pastors of his churches. What this vision gives us is a picture of heaven so that "as it is in heaven, so shall it be on earth." We are invited into the heavenly throne room in order to see what our heavenly pastoral counterparts are doing so that we may follow them in practice here and now. These elders' heavenly presence is a foretaste of our heavenly presence, and their focus prompts us today in where our focus should be.

In a word, the elders of heaven have their gaze locked on the center throne. They are engaged and responsive only to the acting and promptings that emanate from God's presence and work. They are fixated on the one on the throne. As we should be. If we've come to the end of our ropes as pastors and have discovered that we are not enough, then we can follow the gaze of those in heaven to see the one who is more than enough for all of us, for all of our churches, for all of our lives.

The five songs of worship interwoven through Revelation 4–5 help us see clearly the one who is enough for us and give us a clear vision of where our eyes should focus. They are, as it were, a worship liturgy calling us see and respond to the glorious Triune God. We are invited to fix our eyes on him. As we participate in this worship service, we find several focal points of Jesus' glory for us to fix our eyes on.

FIXATE ON HIS HOLINESS

As the heavenly scene unfolds and centers on the throne, we hear the four living creatures perpetually call all of heaven to worship. They proclaim, "Holy, holy, holy, is the Lord God Almighty, who was and is and is to come!" (Rev 4:8). Those in the presence of God have never failed to see or exalt the holiness of God.

God's holiness is his complete transcendence, uniqueness, and purity. He is absolutely distinct from his creatures and superior in every way. As "Lord God Almighty," he is placed in absolute superiority to everything in existence. He is supreme and above all. Furthermore, his holiness is seen in his eternality. That is to say, his holiness will never be diminished. He was, he is, he is to come. There is no shortage of his perfections.

As pastors we need to fixate here first. We aren't called into ministry because we are worthy or because God needed good leaders to move his church forward. He wasn't in need of our powerful rhetorical skills to get his message across. God isn't short on glory worth contemplating forever. To see God as holy, we are reminded that he is the Almighty One! We are not God.

Our attempts to build or grow churches are inconsequential if we put ourselves in the seat of Almighty God. He doesn't need you or me: "Thus says the LORD: 'Heaven is my throne, and the earth is my footstool; what is the house that you would build for me, and what is the place of my rest? All these things my hand has made, and so all these things came to be, declares the LORD. But this is the one to whom I will look: he who is humble and contrite in spirit and trembles at my word'" (Isa 66:1–2).

Fixing our eyes on his holiness places us rightly in humility before him. He is the one to worship, and we are the worshipers. He is the Almighty, and we are servants. All things are from him, and through him, and to him. To him be the glory forever (Rom 11:26)!

FIXATE ON HIS GLORY AS ALL-POWERFUL CREATOR

John notes that "whenever the living creatures give glory and honor and thanks to him who is seated on the throne," the elders respond (Rev 4:9). Specifically they fall down to the ground before him, casting their crowns to his throne. Humility is the posture of the pastor. If we are always attentive to God, we will always have his greatness before us. Consequentially we will also have our finiteness in view, as we should. This is the continual posture of the heavenly pastors. God is always holy; we are always responding to him in worship.

As the call to worship commenced, the heavenly pastors responded with a song of their own: "Worthy are you, our Lord and God, to receive glory and honor and power, for you created all things, and by your will they existed and were created" (Rev 4:11). Fixated on the glory of God, they ascribe worth, glory, honor, and power to his name. God alone is worthy of being made much of. He alone is rightful in being given the highest place of dignity. He alone is ascribed power over all things. All of this is because of who he is.

The elders declare his right to all glory, honor, and power because he is the one who created all things. All things exist because of his divine desire and subsequent ability to carry out those desires. Paul speaks of Christ this way as well: "He is the image of the invisible God, the firstborn of all creation. For by him all things were created, in heaven and on earth, visible and invisible, whether thrones or dominions or rulers or authorities—all things were created through him and for him. And he is before all things, and in him all things hold together" (Col 1:15–17).

For those of us who have planted churches, we can functionally fall prey to the lie that the church exists because we started it. We have shone the light in the darkness of our communities, gathered the people of God, trained leaders, multiplied disciples, and brought about a gospel culture all from our entrepreneurial gifts of leadership and wise implementation of best practices. Even if we aren't founding church planters, we can believe the lie that we are the sustainers of the church. We hold it together by our great sermons, pastoral care, diligent evangelism, and ministry programs designed to connect with a myriad of people. We begin to exalt ourselves as "worthy" because of our creative, sustaining power.

But the heavenly elders will have none of that pride. Rightful worth must be ascribed to the Creator on his throne. He is the one to get glory for his creation of the church. He is the one to be given honor for holding it together. He is the one to be appropriated power as we submit the church to him. Everything is his, after all.

If we as pastors will fix our eyes on him as the omnipotent Creator, we will be sustained by knowing that Jesus' promise to build his church—that "the gates of hell shall not prevail against it"—will come to pass (Matt 16:18). He doesn't need us to see his church be formed, built, sustained, and brought to perfection. He is enough as the all-powerful Creator to call into existence those things that do not exist by the powerful word of his gospel (Rom 1:16–17; 4:17).

FIXATE ON HIS REDEMPTIVE SUFFERING

The heavenly worship service moves forward with John seeing Almighty God with a scroll in his hand and an angel asking who is worthy to open the scroll. No one is found. No one is worthy. No one is able to unfold the redemptive plans of God and execute divine justice and restoration of all things. John is beside himself in grief. Pastoring can feel that way many days. We pray and cry out, "How long, O Lord?" at the injustice and sinful wickedness that pervades this world. We will pray and counsel our people and yet deal with the same struggles and sins year after year. Little spiritual progress seems to be made. Can no one really save us?

Yet one of the heavenly elders sees the solution. He pastors John by speaking the Word of God to him: "Weep no more; behold, the Lion of the tribe of Judah, the Root of David, has conquered, so that he can open the scroll and its seven seals" (Rev 5:5). Scripture has power to comfort the afflicted. It renews the brokenhearted and downcast.

John looks up, and on the very center throne is a "Lamb standing, as though it had been slain" (Rev 5:6). The Lion-Lamb is the one who is worthy to take and open the scrolls. As soon as he receives the scroll from the hand of the Almighty One on the throne, the elders lead in worship once again. This time they lead with "a new song saying, 'Worthy are you to take the scroll and to open its seals, for you were slain, and by your blood you ransomed people for God from every tribe and language and people and nation, and you have made them a kingdom and priests to our God, and they shall reign on the earth'" (vv. 9–10).

The elders sing of his worth to carry out the final consummation of all things by his sacrificial atonement. He can bring about the full and right judgment of God on the nations and the final glorification of his people by his suffering and sacrificial death. He ransoms some from every nation by the cross. He is the Savior of his church.

Fixing our eyes on the cross as pastors repudiates our attempts to be the church's Savior and Messiah. We are the friend of the bridegroom pointing the bride to her husband. We see Jesus' suffering and death on our behalf as our only hope of redemption, and we cease promoting alternative means of salvation by religious imitations. We stop attempting to get the church to love us and deem us worthy because of our sacrifice, and show them the real Savior who bled and died for his bride.

Fixing our eyes on his redemptive suffering renews our vision that he actually saves, and he saves *us*. We are reminded that it was his blood that was shed for our sins, his blood that was poured out for our failures as pastors. He died to ransom us for God, putting to death our attempts to earn our own status or position before God by our great pastoring. He has made us "a kingdom and priests to our God" and we "shall reign on the earth" by virtue of his shed blood, not our own. We can die to our own greatness, our own sufficiency, our own pride. Our eyes are fixed on Christ, who is enough to rescue us from our greatest failures, our worst sermons, our poor counseling, our weak prayers, and our deepest sorrows. Christ died for us! He is enough for us.

FIXATE ON HIM

As the force of the accomplishment of Christ's redemptive work stands out in heaven, it brings everyone and everything into worship. The living creatures, the elders, and an innumerable heavenly host proclaim, "with a loud voice, 'Worthy is the Lamb who was slain, to receive power and wealth and wisdom and might and honor and glory and blessing!'" (v. 12).

This fourth song of heaven is a song specifically declaring Christ as worthy for who he is. The Lamb who was slain is worthy in and of himself of all forms of exaltation. His divine excellence is sufficient enough for all our lives. John Calvin said it this way:

> We see that our whole salvation and all its parts are comprehended in Christ. We should therefore take care not to derive the least portion of it from anywhere else. If we seek salvation, we are taught by the very name of Jesus that it is "of him." If we seek any other gifts of the Spirit, they will be found in his anointing. If we seek strength, it lies in his dominion; if purity, in his conception; if gentleness, it appears in his birth. For by his birth he was made like us in all respects that he might learn to feel our pain. If we seek redemption, it lies in his passion; if acquittal, in his condemnation; if remission of the curse, in his cross; if satisfaction, in his sacrifice; if purification, in his blood; if reconciliation, in his descent into hell; if mortification of the flesh, in his tomb; if newness of life, in his resurrection; if immortality, in the same; if inheritance of the Heavenly Kingdom, in his entrance into heaven; if protection, if security, if abundant supply of all blessings, in his Kingdom; if untroubled expectation of judgment, in the power given to him to judge. In short, since rich store of every kind of good abounds in him, let us drink our fill from this fountain, and from no other.[71]

Pastor, fix your eyes on Christ! He is worthy enough to receive all things. We must ascribe to him all our power. It is from his hand that we have leadership. We must ascribe to him all wealth. What do we have that we did not receive (1 Cor 4:7)? Value comes from him, not us. Jesus is wisdom. We humble ourselves to his Word. He is the one who is strong; we are weak. He is the dignified and exalted Lord. We are servants doing our duty. He gets all glory. He receives all blessing. Friends, it's all his!

In the City Church of Wittenberg, Germany, behind the altar, is a painting by one of Martin Luther's friends, Lucas Cranach. In the painting, on the far right-hand side, Luther is seen in a pulpit, preaching. He has the Bible open, his left hand resting on the text, as if to signify everything he says must come from the book. With his right hand he is pointing. His eyes are up, looking.

On the far left-hand side is the congregation: men, women, children, babies. There the congregation is listening, taking in what Luther is saying. But if you follow the direction of their eyes, most of them are not looking at Luther. A few have eyes turned away, looking at other members of the congregation, some with scorn in their face. However, the majority of the congregation is looking up to the center of the painting.

The part of the painting that grabs our attention immediately and fixes our gaze is in the middle: Christ crucified is the center of the work. Luther looks and points to Christ from the Scriptures. The people fix their gaze on Jesus. We see Jesus.

I love this painting because it illustrates the work of a pastor, as much as it does the work of the congregation. As I've heard one pastor say on occasion, "All eyes up! All eyes on Jesus!"[72] Take more long looks at Jesus to sustain you in ministry. Get your eyes off yourself. Look at his all-surpassing glory. Worship him.

The final song is a benediction. It sets up the rest of the book, but again postures us to fix our eyes on God. Every creature in heaven and on earth and under the earth and in the sea, and all that is in them proclaim, "To him who sits on the throne and to the Lamb be blessing and honor and glory and might forever and ever!" (Rev 5:13)

All things are kneeling before the Lord and declaring, "You are enough!"

BECAUSE PASTORS BELONG TO JESUS, JESUS IS ENOUGH

Pastor, that is our bright future. That is our heavenly reality right now. We would be wise to follow the lead of our heavenly pastors and fall down and worship. That is what pastoring is: worship. Keeping people attentive to Christ, who is enough for all things at all times in every way. But that isn't just true for our churches; it's true for pastors like you and me who need someone to be enough for us.

Jesus is that one. Jesus is enough.

Blessed Lord Jesus,
You say you hold your pastors in your hand,
nothing in all the universe will separate us from your love.
Lead us in remembering our union with you.
Grant us the grace and humility to hear and believe that
you are more than enough for us.
Give us confidence to shepherd the flock of God with
your word, by your powerful Spirit.
Build, strengthen, and sustain your church, which you
bought by your blood.
We pray this in your name,
who lives and reigns with the Father and the Holy Spirit,
one God now and forever.
Amen.

ACKNOWLEDGMENTS

T his book has been the product of more than just a few years in my life. It's been a lived experience for at least twenty. Yet in the last several years there has been a growing community who have invested deeply in seeing this project come to completion. I am deeply grateful for their support.

Thank you to Jonathan Dodson who has constantly encouraged me to write, and has entrusted the stewardship of Gospel-Centered Discipleship (gcdiscipleship.com) into my leadership. Your encouragement has encouraged me to keep going and keep laboring as a writer.

Thanks to Erik Wolgemuth for your perseverance in taking me on, helping refine my ideas, and representing me so well. Let's do it again!

I'm exceedingly grateful to Josh Carrillo for reading each chapter and giving me real-time feedback. I couldn't have asked for a closer and better friend! Nathan Didlake supported me in providing suggestions and helpful edits borne out of his experience. I am grateful.

Todd Hains has been an amazing editor to work with on this project and I am utterly indebted to him for his patience, wisdom, and willingness to serve me and the pastors I am writing for. The entire team at Lexham Press has been astounding and I couldn't imagine working with a better group on this project. Thank you all!

A church stands behind this project as well, to whom I am grateful for their support, prayers, and love. I deeply appreciate and love the campus pastors at Woodside who have provided the community and brotherhood that has helped shape my encouragement in this book. To the congregation at Woodside Plymouth, thank you for loving, praying, and pursuing Jesus with me. It's my joy to be your pastor.

Pastoral ministry is learned mainly from observation and experience. Having godly and faithful mentors to learn from is a gift of God's grace. Pastor Chris Bauer has been that mentor who walked with me through so many of my formative years of ministry in Santa Rosa, California. I wouldn't know how to pastor as I do had you not shown me the ropes. Thank you.

Stephanie, you have sacrificed more than anyone else to see this book come to fruition. Thank you for staying in my corner through the challenges brought our way for the duration of this project. Your love, prayers, encouragement, support, freeing up time, and caring for me through the season this book was written are gifts that I can only hope to repay with my love and devotion. Let's live right on. I love you!

Allison and Ethan, thanks for letting and encouraging dad to write. You're the best.

Finally, to the All-Sufficient One, Jesus Christ, who is for me all things. To you be all glory! May this book be an outflowing of worship and devotion to you and a means of helping your shepherds in the church flourish. I owe you all.

ENDNOTES

1   Prayer adapted from John Calvin and the Collect for the Fourth Sunday after Easter. See John Calvin, *Commentaries on the Minor Prophets*, 5 vols., trans. John Owen (Calvin Translation Society, 1846–1849), 5:164; Samuel L. Bray and Drew Nathaniel Keane, eds., *The 1662 Book of Common Prayer: International Edition* (IVP Academic, 2021), 147–48

2   See John Piper, *Don't Waste Your Life*, in *The Collected Works of John Piper*, ed. Justin Taylor and David Mathis (Crossway, 2017), 5, 421.

3   Peter J. Leithart, *Revelation 1–11*, International Theological Commentary on the Holy Scripture of the Old and New Testaments (Bloomsbury T&T Clark, 2018), 123.

4   Augustine, *On Christian Teaching*, trans. R. P. H. Green (Oxford University Press, 1997), 21.

5   Leon Morris, *Revelation: An Introduction and Commentary*, Tyndale New Testament Commentaries (InterVarsity Press, 1987), 64.

6   Harold L. Senkbeil, *The Care of Souls: Cultivating a Pastor's Heart* (Lexham, 2019).

7   See Chuck DeGroat's book *When Narcissism Comes to Church* (InterVarsity Press, 2020), or Christianity Today's podcast *The Rise and Fall of Mars Hill*, 2021.

8   See J. Oswald Sanders, *Spiritual Leadership, Spiritual Discipleship, Spiritual Maturity* (Moody Press, 2017).

9   James K. A. Smith, *You Are What You Love: The Spiritual Power of Habit* (Brazos, 2016), 20–21.

10 J. I. Packer, *The Gospel in the Prayer Book* (InterVarsity Press, 2021), https://www.ivpress.com/Media/Default/Content-Articles/Packer-Gospel-in-the-Prayer-Book.pdf.

11 I heard John Starke share this at the Harbor Network Leaders' Summit on October 13, 2021, in Louisville, KY.

12 Sam Storms, "Living with One Foot Raised: Calvin on the Glory of the Final Resurrection & Heaven," in *With Calvin in the Theater of God: The Glory of Christ and Everyday Life*, ed. John Piper and David Mathis (Crossway, 2010), 114.

13   Mark Galli and Ted Olsen, introduction to *131 Christians Everyone Should Know* (Broadman & Holman, 2000), 18.

14   Ian Paul, *Revelation: An Introduction and Commentary*, Tyndale New Testament Commentaries (InterVarsity Press, 2018), 83.

15   David Seal, "Smyrna," in *The Lexham Bible Dictionary*, ed. John D. Barry et al. (Lexham, 2016).

16   Alexander Roberts, James Donaldson, and A. Cleveland Coxe, eds., *Martyrdom of Polycarp*, in ANF (Christian Literature Company, 1885), 1:41.

17   Interestingly they tried to nail him down but he requested to be left alone stating, "Leave me as I am; for He that giveth me strength to endure the fire, will also enable me; without your securing me by nails, to remain without moving in the pile." *Martyrdom of Polycarp*, 1:42.

18   *Martyrdom of Polycarp*, 1:42.

19   Martin Luther, "Selected Sermons," in *The Annotated Luther*, vol. 4, *Pastoral Writings*, ed. Mary Jane Haemig (Fortress, 2016), 61.

20   Eugene Peterson, *A Long Obedience in the Same Direction: Discipleship in an Instant Society* (InterVarsity Press, 2000).

21   Jim Elliot, *The Journals of Jim Elliot*, ed. Elisabeth S. Elliot (Fleming H Revell, 1983), 174.

22   Eugene H. Peterson, *Working the Angles: The Shape of Pastoral Integrity* (Eerdmans, 1987), 1.

23   Peterson, *Working the Angles*, 2.

24   Peterson, *Working the Angles*, 2.

25   J. C. Ryle, *Holiness: Its Nature, Hindrances, Difficulties and Roots* (William Hunt, 1889), 399.

26   Grant R. Osborne, *Revelation*, Baker Exegetical Commentary on the New Testament (Baker Academic, 2002), 140.

27   Abraham Kuyper, "Sphere Sovereignty," in *Abraham Kuyper: A Centennial Reader*, ed. James D. Bratt (Eerdmans, 1998), 488.

28   Quoted in Külli Tõniste, "Pergamum," in *The Lexham Bible Dictionary*, ed. John D. Barry et al. (Lexham, 2016).

29   David A. deSilva, "The Social and Geographical World of Pergamum (Revelation 1:11; 2:12–17)," in *Lexham Geographic Commentary on Acts through Revelation*, ed. Barry J. Beitzel, Jessica Parks, and Doug Mangum, Lexham Geographic Commentary (Lexham, 2019), 653.

30   Osborne, *Revelation*, 144.

31   Duane F. Watson, "Nicolaitans," in *The Anchor Yale Bible Dictionary*, ed. David Noel Freedman (Doubleday, 1992), 1106–7.

32   Martin Luther, *Lectures on Genesis, Chapters 26 to 30*, ed. Jaroslav Pelikan, *Luther's Works* 5 (Concordia, 1968), 123.

33 See Mark Sayers,
    World will Create a Remnant of Renewed Christian Leaders (Moody, 2022).

34 Gordon D. Fee, *Revelation*, New Covenant Commentary Series (Cascade, 2011), 38.

35 Thanks to a fellow campus pastor at Woodside, Billy Creech, for giving me this analogy.

36 Author's translation.

37 Johannes P. Louw and Eugene Albert Nida, *Greek-English Lexicon of the New Testament: Based on Semantic Domains* (United Bible Societies, 1996), 163.

38 Lynsey M. Barron and William P. Eiselstein, "Report of Independent Investigation into Sexual Misconduct of Ravi Zacharias," February 9, 2021, https://s3-us-west-2.amazonaws.com/rzimmedia.rzim.org/assets/downloads/Report-of-Investigation.pdf.

39 This saying is attributed to Nicholas Ludwig von Zinzendorf.

40 This is the subtitle of Sally Llyod-Jones's tremendous book *The Jesus Storybook Bible* (Zonderkids, 2007). As it walks through the major stories of the Bible it shows the centrality of Christ as the theme of all Scripture.

41 This is the title of Eugene Peterson's classic work on discipleship.

42 Senkbeil, *The Care of Souls*, 184.

43 Senkbeil, *The Care of Souls*, 191

44 John Owen, *The Works of John Owen*, ed. William H. Goold (T&T Clark, n.d.), 6:9.

45 Osborne, *Revelation*, 167.

46 Leithart, *Revelation*, 179.

47 Thomas R. Schreiner, "Revelation," in *ESV Expository Commentary*, vol. 12, *Hebrews–Revelation*, ed. Iain M. Duguid, James M. Hamilton Jr., and Jay Sklar (Crossway, 2018), 586.

48 Osborne, *Revelation*, 171.

49 John Kleinig, *Grace upon Grace: Spirituality for Today* (Concordia), 11.

50 William C. Weinrich, ed., *Revelation*, Ancient Christian Commentary on Scripture, NT 12 (InterVarsity Press, 2005), 40.

51 C. H. Spurgeon, *Lectures to My Students: A Selection from Addresses Delivered to the Students of the Pastors' College, Metropolitan Tabernacle*, (London: Passmore and Alabaster, 1875), 1:4.

52 Martin Luther, "The Invocavit Sermons," ed. Martin J. Lohrmann, in *The Annotated Luther*, vol. 4, *Pastoral Writings*, ed. Mary Jane Haemig (Fortress, 2016), 22 (emphasis added).

53 Compline collect from Lutheran Service Book.

54 Daniel J. Thorpe, "Philadelphia," in *The Lexham Bible Dictionary*, ed. John D. Barry et al. (Lexham, 2016).

55 Thorpe, "Philadelphia."

56 Robert H. Mounce, *The Book of Revelation*, New International Commentary on the New Testament (Eerdmans, 1997), 98.

57 Mounce, *The Book of Revelation*, 99.

58 C. S. Lewis, "The Inner Ring," in *The Weight of Glory* (Harper San Francisco, 2001), 141–57.

59 Lewis, "The Inner Ring," 147.

60 "The Jews in Philadelphia had probably taken advantage of their privileged civic status and told the Roman authorities that Christians were not truly Jews, thereby exposing them to persecution from the state, presumably because of their refusal to participate in the imperial cult. Jews received a special exemption from Rome, but the same exemption was not given to Christianity, a new and strange movement." Thomas R. Schreiner, "Revelation," 590.

61 Author's paraphrase.

62 Francis A. Schaeffer, *The Complete Works of Francis A. Schaeffer: A Christian Worldview* (Crossway, 1982), 3:9.

63 Mounce, *The Book of Revelation*, 105.

64 Osborne, *Revelation*, 205.

65 M. J. S. Rudwick and C. J. Hemer, "Laodicea," *New Bible Dictionary*, ed. D. R. W. Wood et al. (InterVarsity Press, 1996), 672.

66 I've never known of a group that would have this conversation and someone own up to lying because of the last question asked. Never mind that the man asking the question probably had little to no equipping on how to respond.

67 Derek Webb, "I Want a Broken Heart," *I See Things Upside Down* (INO Records, 2004).

68 Richard Sibbes, *The Complete Works of Richard Sibbes*, ed. Alexander Balloch Grosart (James Nichol; James Nisbet; W. Robertson, 1862), 47.

69 See Senkbeil, *The Care of Souls*, chap. 11, for helpful insight into finding a pastor to pastor you.

70 *Presbyteros*: 1 Tim 5:17, 19; Titus 1:5; Jas 5:14; 1 Pet 5:1.

71 John Calvin, *Institutes of the Christian Religion*, ed. John T. McNeill, trans. Ford Lewis Battles, Library of Christian Classics (repr. Westminster John Knox Press, 2011), 1:527–28.

72 Adapted from my article "All Eyes on Jesus," *Gospel-Centered Discipleship*, July 16, 2019, https://gcdiscipleship.com/article-feed/2019/7/16/all-eyes-on-jesus.

WORKS CITED

Augustine. *On Christian Teaching*. Translated by R. P. H. Green. Oxford University Press, 1997.

Barron, Lynsey M., and William P. Eiselstein. "Report of Independent Investigation into Sexual Misconduct of Ravi Zacharias." https://s3-us-west-2.amazonaws.com/rzimmedia.rzim.org/assets/downloads/Report-of-Investigation.pdf. February 9, 2021.

Bray, Samuel L., and Drew Nathaniel Keane, eds. *The 1662 Book of Common Prayer: International Edition*. Downers Grove, IL: IVP Academic, 2021.

Calvin, John. *Commentaries on the Minor Prophets, John Calvin*. Translated by John Owen. Calvin Translation Society, 1846–1949.

Calvin, John. *Institutes of the Christian Religion*. Edited by John T. McNeill. Translated by Ford Lewis Battles. John Knox Press, 2011.

Cosper, Mike. "Who Killed Mars Hill?" June 21, 2021, in *The Rise and Fall of Mars Hill*, produced by Mike Cosper and Joy Beth Smith, podcast, https://www.christianitytoday.com/ct/podcasts/rise-and-fall-of-mars-hill.

Coxe, A. Cleveland, James Donaldson, and Alexander Roberts, eds. "Martyrdom of Polycarp." *The Ante-Nicene Fathers*. Christian Literature Company, 1885.

DeGroat, Chuck. *When Narcissism Comes to Church*. InterVarsity Press, 2020.

deSilva, David A. "The Social and Geographical World of Pergamum." *Lexham Geographic Commentary on Acts Through Revelation.*, eds. Bary J. Beitzel, Jessica Parks, and Doug Mangum. Lexham Press, 2019.

Duguid, Iain M., James M. Hamilton, Jr., and Jay Sklar, eds. "Revelation." *ESV Expository Commentary volume 12, Hebrews–Revelation*. Crossway, 2018.

Elliot, Elisabeth, ed. *The Journals of Jim Elliot*. Fleming H. Revell, 1983.

Fee, Gordon D., *Revelation*. Cascade, 2011.

Galli, Mark, and Ted Olsen. *131 Christians Everyone Should Know*. Broadman & Holman, 2000.

Kleinig, John. *Grace Upon Grace: Spirituality for Today*. Concordia, 2008.

Kuyper, Abraham. "Sphere Sovereignty." *Abraham Kuyper: A Centennial Reader*, ed. James D. Bratt. Eerdmans, 1998.

Leithart, Peter J. "Revelation 1–11." *International Theological Commentary on the Holy Scriptures of the Old and New Testaments.* Bloomsbury T&T Clark, 2018.

Lewis, C. .S. "The Inner Ring." *The Weight of Glory.* Harper, 2001.

Lloyd-Jones, Sally. *The Jesus Storybook Bible.* Zondervan, 2007.

Louw, Johannes P., and Eugene Albert Nida. *Greek-English Lexicon of the New Testament: Based on Semantic Domains.* United Bible Societies, 1996.

Luther, Martin. *Lectures on Genesis, Chapters 26 to 30,* ed. Jaroslav Pelikan. Concordia, 1968.

Luther, Martin. "Selected Sermons." *The Annotated Luther volume 4,* ed. Mary Jane Haemig. Fortress, 2016.

Luther, Martin. The Invocavit Sermons." *The Annotated Luther volume 4,* ed. Mary Jane Haemig. Fortress, 2016.

Mathis, David, and Justin Taylor. "Don't Waste Your Life." *The Collected Works of John Piper.* Crossway, 2017.

Morris, Leon. *Revelation: An Introduction and Commentary.* InterVarsity Press, 1987.

Mounce, Robert H. "The Book of Revelation." *New International Commentary on the New Testament.* Eerdmans, 1997.

Osborne, Grant R. *Revelation.* Baker Academic, 2002.

Owen, John. *The Works of John Owen,* ed. William H. Goold. T&T Clark, n.d.

Packer, J. I. *The Gospel in the Prayer Book.* InterVarsity Press, 2021.

Paul, Ian. *Revelation: An Introduction and Commentary.* InterVarsity Press, 2018.

Peterson, Eugene H. *A Long Obedience in the Same Direction: Discipleship in an Instant Society.* InterVarsity Press, 2000.

Peterson, Eugene H. *Working the Angles: The Shape of Pastoral Integrity.* Eerdmans, 1987.

Ryle, J. C. *Holiness: Its Nature, Hindrances, Difficulties, and Roots.* William Hunt, 1889.

Sanders, J. Oswald. *Spiritual Leadership, Spiritual Discipleship, Spiritual Maturity.* Moody Press, 2017.

Schaeffer, Francis A. *The Complete Works of Francis A. Schaeffer: A Christian Worldview.* Crossway, 1982.

Seal, David. "Smyrna." *The Lexham Bible Dictionary,* ed. John D. Barry. Lexham Press, 2016.

Senkbeil, Harold L. *The Care of Souls: Cultivating a Pastor's Heart.* Lexham Press, 2019.

Sibbes, Richard. *The Complete Works of Richard Sibbes,* ed. Alexander Balloch Grosart. James Nichol, James Nisbet and W. Robertson, 1862.

Smith, James K. A. *You are What You Love: The Spiritual Power of Habit.* Brazos, 2016.

Spurgeon, C. H. *Lectures to My Students: A Selection from Addresses Delivered to the Students of the Pastors' College, Metropolitan Tabernacle.* Passmore and Alabaster, 1875.

Storms, Sam. "Living with One Foot Raised: Calvin on the Glory of the Final Resurrection and Heaven." *With Calvin in the Theater of God: The Glory of Christ and Everyday Life.* Crossway, 2010.

Thorpe, Daniel J. "Philadelphia." *The Lexham Bible Dictionary*, ed. John D. Barry. Lexham Press, 2016.

Tõniste, Külli. "Pergamum." *The Lexham Bible Dictionary,* ed. John D. Barry. Lexham Press, 2016.

Watson, Duane F. "Nicolaitans." *The Anchor Yale Bible Dictionary*, ed. David Noel Freedman. Doubleday, 1992.

Webb, Derek. "I Want a Broken Heart." *I See Things Upside Down.* INO Records, 2004.

Weinrich, William C. *Revelation: Ancient Christian Commentary on Scripture.* InterVarsity Press, 2005.

Wood. D. R. W., I. Howard Marshall, eds. "Laodicea." *New Bible Dictionary.* Intervarsity Press, 1996.

Writebol, Jeremy. "All Eyes on Jesus." *Gospel-Centered Discipleship.* https://gcdiscipleship.com/article-feed/2019/7/16/all-eyes-on-jesus. July 16, 2019.

SCRIPTURE INDEX

OLD TESTAMENT

NEW TESTAMENT